# PREFACE

## 1. Scope

This publication provides joint doctrine for homeland defense across the range of military operations. It provides information on planning, command and control, interorganizational coordination, and operations required to defeat external threats to, and aggression against, the homeland, or against other threats as directed by the President.

## 2. Purpose

This publication has been prepared under the direction of the Chairman of the Joint Chiefs of Staff (CJCS). It sets forth joint doctrine to govern the activities and performance of the Armed Forces of the United States in joint homeland defense operations and provides the guidance for US military coordination with other US Government departments and agencies during operations and for US military involvement in multinational operations supporting homeland defense. It provides military guidance for the exercise of authority by combatant commanders and other joint force commanders (JFCs) and prescribes joint doctrine for operations, education, and training. It provides military guidance for use by the Armed Forces in preparing their appropriate plans. It is not the intent of this publication to restrict the authority of the JFC from organizing the force and executing the mission in a manner the JFC deems most appropriate to ensure unity of effort in the accomplishment of the overall objective.

## 3. Application

a. Joint doctrine established in this publication applies to the Joint Staff, commanders of combatant commands, subunified commands, joint task forces, subordinate components of these commands, combat support agencies, and the Services.

b. The guidance in this publication is authoritative; as such, this doctrine will be followed except when, in the judgment of the commander, exceptional circumstances dictate otherwise. If conflicts arise between the contents of this publication and the contents of Service publications, this publication will take precedence unless the CJCS, normally in coordination with the other members of the Joint Chiefs of Staff, has provided more current and specific guidance. Commanders of forces operating as part of a multinational (alliance or coalition) military command should follow multinational doctrine and procedures ratified by the US. For doctrine and procedures not ratified by the US, commanders should evaluate and follow the multinational command's doctrine and procedures, where applicable and consistent with US law, regulations, and doctrine.

For the Chairman of the Joint Chiefs of Staff:

CURTIS M. SCAPARROTTI
Lieutenant General, U.S. Army
Director, Joint Staff

Intentionally Blank

# SUMMARY OF CHANGES
## REVISION OF JOINT PUBLICATION 3-27
### DATED 12 JULY 2007

- **Restructures document format; moves key sections from appendices and other chapters for a more appropriate flow.**

- **Clarifies and elaborates on the similarities, differences, and integration of homeland defense (HD), homeland security, and defense support of civil authorities.**

- **Includes new, updated, and emerging threats in the discussion of the homeland threat environment.**

- **Defines and clarifies the domestic use of rules of engagement and rules for the use of force in HD operations.**

- **Highlights importance of information sharing between key players and the ability of the commander to tailor interagency coordination.**

- **Adds cyberspace as a domain within the information environment, where HD operations will occur instead of including it in "combat supporting operations."**

- **Clarifies and elaborates thoroughly the role of planning for cyberspace operations and the duties involved.**

- **Provides greater depth on command and control and relationships.**

- **Adds and elaborates on specific protections such as missiles, missile defenses, and the coordination/integration of these assets.**

- **Establishes force protection as a critical area along with antiterrorism and force health protection measures.**

- **Updates reference and acronyms.**

Intentionally Blank

# TABLE OF CONTENTS

GLOSSARY

FIGURE

# EXECUTIVE SUMMARY
## COMMANDER'S OVERVIEW

- **Provides an overview of homeland defense policy and legal considerations.**

- **Describes command relationships and interorganizational coordination for homeland defense.**

- **Explains homeland defense planning and operational considerations.**

- **Describes relationships between homeland security, homeland defense, and defense support of civil authorities.**

- **Discusses how unified action develops unity of effort.**

- **Explains special considerations for joint functions in homeland defense operations.**

---

## Fundamentals of Homeland Defense Operations

*Homeland Defense (HD) is the protection of US sovereignty, territory, domestic population, and critical infrastructure against external threats and aggression, or other threats as directed by the President.*

The US homeland is the physical region that includes the continental United States, Alaska, Hawaii, US territories, and surrounding territorial waters and airspace. The homeland is a functioning theater of operations, and the Department of Defense (DOD) regularly performs a wide range of defense operations within the theater. DOD is responsible for the homeland defense (HD) mission, and leads the response with support from international partners and United States Government (USG) departments and agencies.

The homeland operational environments require pre-event and ongoing coordination with interagency and multinational partners to integrate capabilities and facilitate unified action. DOD plans and prepares to operate in concert with other USG entities.

*HD, Defense Support of Civil Authorities and Homeland Security*

HD, defense support to civil authorities (DSCA), and homeland security (HS) operations or events may occur simultaneously. The Department of Homeland Security is the lead federal agency for HS. HS is a concerted national effort to prevent terrorist attacks within the US; reduce domestic vulnerability to terrorism, major disasters, and other emergencies; and minimize the damage and recover from attacks, major disasters, and other emergencies that occur.

DSCA is support provided by US federal military forces, DOD civilians, DOD contract personnel, DOD component assets, and National Guard (NG) forces in response to requests for assistance from civil authorities for domestic emergencies, law enforcement (LE) support, and other domestic activities, or from qualifying entities for special events.

*Threats*

The homeland is confronted by a variety of disparate and interrelated threats that demand coordinated procedures and synchronized efforts among interagency partners responsible for LE and national defense, particularly those who have overlapping roles, responsibilities, authorities, and capabilities.

*HD Policy and Legal Considerations*

Multiple documents provide guidance for conducting HD operations. Certain functions, such as intelligence activities, military information support operations, rules of engagement, and rules for the use of force, have specific applications and legal implications when conducted domestically.

*Posse Comitatus Act*

The Posse Comitatus Act (PCA) prohibits the use of military personnel from performing various functions within the homeland. However, when directed by the President, the use of military operations for HD is a constitutional exception to the PCA. When performing HD operations, Title 10, United States Code, forces are not subject to the restriction of the PCA.

*Intelligence Activities*

Intelligence activities conducted by US intelligence organizations in the US and its territories are strictly controlled. Several regulations and laws specifically govern the use of DOD intelligence assets and organizations in domestic operations.

*Rules of Engagement (ROE) and Rules for the Use of Force (RUF)*

The Chairman of the Joint Chiefs of Staff Instruction 3121.01B, Standing Rules of

*Commanders are responsible for the education of their personnel on ROE and RUF and their training on the use of nonlethal and lethal force.*

*Engagement/Standing Rules for the Use of Force for US Forces,* establishes fundamental policies and procedures that govern the actions taken by US military commanders and personnel during global DOD operations, including HD operations.

The standing rules of engagement (SROE) applies during all military operations, contingencies, and routine military functions occurring outside the US and its territories for mission accomplishment and the exercise of self-defense. SROE does not apply to air and maritime HD missions conducted within the US and its territories or territorial seas, unless otherwise directed by the Secretary of Defense (SecDef).

The standing rules for the use of force apply to land HD missions occurring within US territory and to DOD forces, civilians, and contractors performing LE and security duties at all DOD installations (and off-installation, while conducting official DOD security functions),within or outside US territory, unless otherwise directed by SecDef.

*The Strategy for HD and Civil Support calls for securing against attack through an active, layered defense.*

This defense strategy seamlessly integrates US capabilities in the forward regions of the world, in the geographic approaches to US territory, and within the US homeland.

In the forward regions, the objective is to detect, deter, prevent, or when necessary, defeat threats to the US. Actions may include combat operations, military engagement activities, peace operations, or preemptive measures such as direct action missions, cyberspace operations, or global strike.

The approaches extend from the limits of the homeland to the forward regions. The primary objective of actions within the approaches is to locate threats as far from the homeland as possible and defeat them at a safe distance. The National Military Strategy (NMS) emphasizes the importance of joining the efforts of multinational partners and intragency partners to form an integrated defense.

In the event that defeating threats in forward regions and approaches fails, DOD must be postured to take immediate, decisive action to defend against and defeat the threat in the homeland. Actions in the homeland may take place simultaneously and in coordination with operations conducted in the forward regions and/or the approaches.

*The HD Operational Framework*

DOD conducts activities and operations globally intended to contribute to the defense of the homeland. They are carried out in various operational environments, including the air, land, maritime, and space domains and the information environment (which includes cyberspace). The information environment is also considered distinct, but it includes cyberspace and resides within the physical domains. HD operations require active and passive defenses, and DOD may conduct offensive actions (to include preemptive activities) to deter, disrupt, and destroy adversary capabilities before they can be offensively employed.

## Command Relationships and Interorganizational Coordination

*Unified Action*

Unified action synchronizes, coordinates, and/or integrates joint, single-Service, and multinational operations with the activities of other interagency partners, nongovernmental organizations (NGOs), intergovernmental organizations (IGOs), and the private sector to achieve unity of effort.

*Command and Control Relationships and Responsibilities*

Military forces will remain under the control of the established chain of command when conducting HD operations. In exceptional circumstances and in accordance with established DOD policies, NG forces may conduct HD activities while in state active duty status.

United States Northern Command (USNORTHCOM) and US Pacific Command have specified tasks for HD activities. They are responsible for planning, organizing, and executing HD operations within their respective areas of responsibility (AORs). The other combatant commands support them and contribute to the protection of the US homeland either through actions within their own AOR (forward regions and approaches) or through global responsibilities assigned in the Unified Command Plan.

*Interagency Coordination*

During a HD operation, civil authorities continue to operate and perform many of their respective routine functions. HS activities of some interagency partners may overlap with some HD activities, and while the major military activities that are the responsibilities of DOD cannot be accomplished by other interagency partners, their support is essential. Unity of effort among all HD participants is fundamental and essential. HD operations are conducted in a complex operational environment that contains thousands of different jurisdictions (federal, state, tribal, and local), many agencies and organizations, and several allies and multinational partners. From a USG perspective, this necessitates coordinated and integrated activities, that have been previously exercised/rehearsed to facilitate effective interagency interoperability in addition to unity of effort.

*Multinational Forces*

To conduct the full range of HD operations, combatant commanders should consider all instruments of national power—military, diplomatic, economic, and informational, as well as multinational and nonmilitary organizations. When a response force resides within an alliance, the procedures and structure of that alliance will normally determine the operational level leadership. When a response force is based in a coalition (or a lead nation structure in an alliance), the designated lead nation will normally select the operational level leadership.

## Planning and Operations for Homeland Defense

*Operational Environmental Factors*

Civil-military relationships may be more complicated during HD operations because the military operations will be taking place in our homeland. Regardless of the size and scope of the particular operations, inevitably they will involve multiple jurisdictions (such as cities, counties, regions, tribes, and states). Managing such relationships will require significant time and effort on the part of federal, state, local, and tribal authorities to ensure proper coordination.

The joint force commanders (JFC's) communications synchronization should support the broader USG effort and closely coordinate and solicit support from other agencies and organizations. The role of public affairs (PA) in HD operations is to support the JFC by communicating truthful and factual unclassified information about DOD activities to US, allied, national, international, and internal audiences. Due to the involvement of other USG departments and agencies in HD missions, military PA will operate in an interagency environment which requires cooperation, coordination, and unity of effort.

**Non-DOD Federal, State, Territorial, Local, and Tribal Planning Factors**

Interorganizational coordination must occur between elements of DOD and non-DOD federal, state, local, and tribal agencies as well as other engaged USG departments and agencies for the purpose of achieving HD objectives.

**Strategic Guidance**

General military planning guidance and strategy are provided in high-level policy documents such as the Defense Strategic Guidance and the NMS. Specific planning factors, requirements, and objectives for HD operations are contained in operational plans and concept plans associated with the mission.

**Intelligence Sharing for Homeland Defense**

Information sharing facilitates intelligence and information sharing environments that should include as many essential participants as possible, understanding that not all are capable of participating in a collaborative environment. When possible, a collaborative intelligence sharing environment should be capable of generating and moving intelligence, operational information, and orders where needed in the shortest possible time.

**Joint Fires**

Joint fires may be provided to assist air, land, maritime, or special operations forces in conducting HD activities within an operational environment framed by complex legal limitations and significant interagency coordination. Although major operations against a major adversarial power remain highly unlikely, various strategic and tactical threats require capabilities and preparations to deter or defeat them.

*Movement and Maneuver in the Conduct of HD*

Large scale HD operations involving maneuver forces, combined arms maneuver and the conduct of major combat offensive or defensive operations would be an extraordinary circumstance involving extraordinary decisions by the President of the US. However, these types of operations are planned and prepared for within the doctrinal realm of HD. HD land defense actions may include: movement and maneuver within the land, sea, or air domains; decisive fires (lethal and nonlethal); closing with and destroying a determined enemy; sustaining a joint force; and setting conditions for a return to peace.

*Protection*

The protection function focuses on conserving the joint force's fighting potential in four primary ways: active defensive measures that protect the joint force, its information, its bases, necessary infrastructure, and lines of communications from an adversary's attack; passive defensive measures that make friendly forces, systems, and facilities difficult to locate, strike, and destroy; application of technology and procedures to reduce the risk of friendly fire; and emergency management and response to reduce the loss of personnel and capabilities due to accidents. It includes, but extends beyond, force protection to encompass protection of US noncombatants; the forces, systems, and civil infrastructure of friendly nations; and other government departments and agencies, IGOs, and NGOs.

*Sustainment*

**Logistics.** Within the USNORTHCOM AOR the Commander of United States Northern Command (CDRUSNORTHCOM) does not have assigned forces and therefore executes operational control or tactical control over attached forces without directive authority for logistics (DAFL). Given the robust logistics capabilities within each Service component and DOD support agency/commercial contracting infrastructure in the USNORTHCOM AOR, DAFL is generally not necessary for CDRUSNORTHCOM to execute the HD mission. **Environmental Considerations.** Military commanders are responsible for employing environmentally responsible practices that minimize adverse impacts to human health and the environment. During all operations, strategies will be developed to reduce or eliminate negative impacts on the environment and to minimize negative impacts to mission accomplishment caused by environmental degradation. Contingency planning for HD must include environmental considerations in planning and executing operations.

## CONCLUSION

This publication provides joint doctrine for planning, command and control, interorganizational coordination, and operations required to defeat external threats to, and aggression against, the homeland, or against other threats as directed by the President.

# CHAPTER I
## FUNDAMENTALS OF HOMELAND DEFENSE OPERATIONS

> *"This nation must have ready forces that can bring victory to our country, and safety to our people...innovative doctrine, strategy, and weaponry...to revolutionize the battlefield of the future and to keep the peace by defining war on our terms...We will build the security of America by fighting our enemies abroad, and protecting our folks here at home."*
>
> **President George W. Bush**
> **10 January 2002 at signing of the 2002 National Defense Appropriations Bill**

## 1. General

a. **The Homeland.** Article I, Section 8 of the US Constitution gives Congress the power to provide for the common defense and authorized the organizing, arming, and disciplining of militia in the service of the U S. The National Security Act of 1947 codified at Title 50, United States Code (USC), Chapter 15, realigned and reorganized the US Armed Forces, foreign policy, and intelligence community (IC) apparatus in the aftermath of World War II. An amendment to the act in 1949, created what we know of as the Department of Defense (DOD) as an executive department in August 1956. The mission of DOD is to provide the military forces needed to deter war and to protect the security of the US. The US employs all instruments of national power to continuously defeat threats to the homeland. DOD executes the homeland defense (HD) mission by detecting, deterring, preventing, and defeating against threats from actors of concern as far forward from the homeland as possible.

b. The US homeland is the physical region that includes the continental United States (CONUS), Alaska, Hawaii, US territories, and surrounding territorial waters and airspace. The homeland is a functioning theater of operations, and the DOD regularly performs a wide range of defense operations within the theater. **HD is the protection of US sovereignty, territory, domestic population, and critical infrastructure against external threats and aggression, or other threats as directed by the President.** An external threat or aggression is an action, incident, or circumstance that originates from outside the boundaries of the homeland. Threats planned, prompted, promoted, caused, or executed by external actors may develop or take place inside the boundaries of the homeland. The reference to external threats does not limit where or how attacks may be planned and executed. DOD is responsible for the HD mission, and leads the response with support from international partners and United States Government (USG) departments and agencies. HD is executed across the active, layered defense construct composed of the forward regions, the approaches, and the homeland.

c. By law, DOD is responsible for two missions in the homeland: HD and defense support of civil authorities (DSCA). DOD organizes a framework of areas of responsibility (AORs) for planning through implementation of the Unified Command Plan (UCP) approved by the President. The UCP establishes the missions and geographic responsibilities for the combatant commands (CCMDs), which execute geographic or functional defense requirements. Two geographic combatant commanders (GCCs) are the supported commanders for HD in their AORs, with virtually all other combatant commanders (CCDRs) supporting them. Commander, United States Northern Command (CDRUSNORTHCOM) and Commander, United States Pacific Command (CDRUSPACOM) are charged with specific responsibilities for HD and DSCA. CDRUSNORTHCOM is responsible for planning, organizing, and, as directed, executing HD operations within the United States Northern Command (USNORTHCOM) AOR in concert with missions performed by the North American Aerospace Defense Command (NORAD). CDRUSPACOM is responsible for planning and, as directed, executing HD operations within the United States Pacific Command (USPACOM) AOR. All other CCDRs, with the exception of Commander, United States Transportation Command (CDRUSTRANSCOM), are responsible for detecting, deterring, and preventing attacks against the US, its territories and bases, and employing appropriate force to defend the Nation in forward regions and within the approaches to the homeland should deterrence fail.

(1) HD, DSCA, and homeland security (HS) operations or events may occur simultaneously. The Department of Homeland Security (DHS) is the lead federal agency (LFA) for HS. HS is a concerted national effort to prevent terrorist attacks within the US; reduce domestic vulnerability to terrorism, major disasters, and other emergencies; and minimize the damage and recover from attacks, major disasters, and other emergencies that occur. HS is typically conducted by federal, state, tribal, and/or local government organizations in conjunction with the private sector; and includes law enforcement (LE) activities related to countering terrorism and other criminal activities. For HS, DOD may conduct DSCA in response to requests for assistance from civil authorities, supporting a lead interagency partner such as DHS or Department of Justice (DOJ), or in some cases, a state governor. DOD support must be formally requested by the applicable civil authority and then approved by the President or Secretary of Defense (SecDef).

*For additional information, see Joint Publication (JP) 3-28,* Defense Support of Civil Authorities.

(2) HD is a DOD mission. DOD is the USG lead agency responsible for defending against traditional external threats or aggression (e.g., nation-state conventional force or weapons of mass destruction [WMD]) attack and against external asymmetric threats. During HD operations, DOD coordinates with other interagency partners that may be undertaking simultaneous operations to counter the same or other threats. The relationship between HS and HD is discussed in more detail in Appendix A, "Relationships Between Homeland Security, Homeland Defense, and Defense Support of Civil Authorities."

(3) The homeland operational environments (both HD and HS) require pre-event and ongoing coordination with interagency and multinational partners to integrate capabilities and facilitate unified action. In this complex environment there are numerous threats across multiple jurisdictions (i.e., federal, state, local, and tribal), that are addressed by a diverse group of actively involved stakeholders to include intergovernmental organizations (IGOs), multinational partnerships, nongovernmental organizations (NGOs), and the private sector. DOD plans and prepares to operate in concert with other USG

entities. For example, DOD operations may coincide with other actions to counter terrorist threats, such as those of a hijacked commercial aircraft or attempts to perpetrate attacks using WMD delivered through air, space, maritime, or land domains. A coordinated approach to unified action promotes early identification of the desired USG objective(s) and subsequent coordination and collaboration with potential participants. Guidance such as the Maritime Operational Threat Response (MOTR) Plan is an example of this approach to operations.

*For additional information see JP 3-08,* Interorganizational Coordination During Joint Operations.

*For information regarding interagency roles, responsibilities, and required coordination protocols for conduct of air defense and maritime security operations to counter threats to the US see the President-approved* Aviation Operational Threat Response (AOTR) Plan and the MOTR Plan.

*Specific guidance on interagency headquarters planning and command center support of HD operations is contained in annex V (Interagency Coordination) of HD concept plans (CONPLANs).*

d. DSCA is support provided by US federal military forces, DOD civilians, DOD contract personnel, DOD component assets, and National Guard (NG) forces (as applicable under Title 10, USC, Section 12304 or Title 32, USC, Section 502) in response to requests for assistance from civil authorities for domestic emergencies, LE support, and other domestic activities, or from qualifying entities for special events. HD and DSCA missions may occur simultaneously and require extensive coordination, integration, and synchronization. Considerations regarding such operations are covered in more detail in Appendix A, "Relationships Between Homeland Security, Homeland Defense, and Defense Support of Civil Authorities."

*For more information on DSCA, see JP 3-28,* Defense Support of Civil Authorities.

e. DOD may also be required to engage in emergency preparedness (EP). EP are measures taken in advance of an emergency to reduce the loss of life and property and to protect a nations institutions from all types of hazards through a comprehensive emergency management program of preparedness, mitigation, response, and recovery. EP is considered a part of DOD's overall preparedness activities. It is not a stand-alone activity, but is an integral part of DOD training, mitigation, and response for both HD and DSCA.

## 2. Threats

a. HD should address all external threats and other threats (as directed by the President) to facilitate a broad-based defense in depth. The USG has sought to shape the international environment through the judicious application of diplomatic, informational, military, and economic instruments of national power. Given the persistent nature of both the traditional nation-state and asymmetric threats, a proactive, comprehensive, and disciplined approach to HD is required. Additionally, military operations conducted in the homeland require an in depth understanding of laws, policies, and procedures because of numerous overlapping jurisdictions and legal limitations of the use of military forces in certain situations.

b. The homeland is confronted by a variety of disparate and interrelated threats that demand coordinated procedures and synchronized efforts among interagency partners responsible for LE and national defense, particularly those who have overlapping roles, responsibilities, authorities, and capabilities. Transnational threats have proven to be complex and enduring. A transnational threat is defined in Title 50, USC, Section 402, as "any transnational activity (including international terrorism, narcotics trafficking, the proliferation of WMD and the delivery systems for such weapons, and organized crime) that threatens the national security of the US." DOD further defines a transnational threat as "any activity, individual, or group not tied to a particular country or region that operates across international boundaries and threatens US national security or interests. These threats also include extremists who enter into convenient relationships that exploit each others' capabilities and cloud the distinction between crime and terrorism (e.g., violent extremist organizations and opportunists, drug trafficking organizations, transnational criminal organizations [TCOs], and those trafficking in persons). Lawless and subversive organizations can take advantage of failed states, contested spaces, and ungoverned areas by forging alliances with corrupt government officials and some foreign intelligence services, further destabilizing political, financial, and security institutions in fragile states, undermining competition in world strategic markets, using cyberspace technologies and other methods to perpetrate sophisticated frauds, creating the potential for the transfer of WMD to terrorists, and expanding narco-trafficking and human and weapons smuggling networks. Figure I-1 lists various aspects of the HD strategic threat environment.

c. **Weapons of Mass Destruction.** Adversaries have and continue to seek WMD and the means to deliver them. US military superiority has deterred nation-states with WMD from using them against the homeland or US forces abroad. However, that same military superiority continues to drive some adversaries to seek asymmetric capabilities, including WMD. These capabilities may enable adversaries to gain a strategic advantage, influence public or political will, and possibly coerce the US, its friends, and allies with the threat of

---

## Homeland Defense Strategic Threat Environment

- Increased capability for cyberspace operations against the United States Government, Department of Defense, and nations' critical infrastructures

- Continued desire of transnational terrorists to attack United States with variety of weapons and means (including chemical, biological, radiological, and nuclear [CBRN]/weapons of mass destruction [WMD])

- Continued proliferation of CBRN/WMD capabilities

- Ongoing rogue nation threats

- Active transnational criminal organizations

- Ongoing illegal immigration/special interest aliens

- Presence of homegrown violent extremists

- Continued traditional threats from nation-states (including intercontinental ballistic missiles)

**Figure I-1. Homeland Defense Strategic Threat Environment**

large-scale destruction. To compound this threat, the technology associated with WMD has proliferated globally as information has become more accessible. Despite counterproliferation and arms control efforts, the capabilities with which adversaries can employ WMD against the US or its interests have increased. A chemical, biological, radiological, and nuclear (CBRN) attack may occur in a variety of forms, from release through conventional means such as a ballistic missile to asymmetric means (e.g., a suitcase radiological device). The risk of terrorist (state and non-state sponsored) and traditional nation-state attacks remain.

*See JP 3-40,* Countering Weapons of Mass Destruction, *for more information on WMD. See JP 3-41,* Chemical, Biological, Radiological, and Nuclear Consequence Management, *for more information on DOD actions and capabilities to mitigate the effects of a CBRN attack.*

d. **Adversaries.** The complex, uncertain, and volatile threat environment, coupled with the number of adversaries that threaten the homeland and US interests abroad, presents the US with a resource-intensive challenge. The world appears smaller, due to the advancement in modern weapons and the increased availability of information. A number of regional powers and non-state actors possess the capability to challenge the interests of the US and its allies. Adversaries take advantage of technology and employ it to move money, communicate with cells in their organizations, approve missions, or conduct intelligence, surveillance, and reconnaissance (ISR) missions on potential targets. They are also using advances in technology to wage propaganda campaigns and various forms of cyberspace attacks against the US and its allies. Some terrorist organizations have grown more extreme in their objectives and actions, and have demonstrated willingness and desire to attack innocent civilians and public infrastructure to further their objectives. Some groups have attained a considerable degree of financial independence with little regard as to the consequences associated with an attack on the US enemies will continue to employ a variety of tactics, in particular, asymmetric employment of weapons, platforms, and information that could significantly affect not only the politico-military balance, but potentially more significant, the US economy and global trade.

e. **The influx of illegal immigrants, special interest aliens, drugs, and contraband pose a possible threat to the homeland.** TCOs have established networks to move people, drugs, or other contraband into the homeland. While primarily HS issues, there are HD implications, because such networks can also be used by terrorists who want to conduct violent acts. TCOs are expanding and diversifying their activities, resulting in the convergence of threats that were once distinct and that could have explosive and destabilizing effects. Securing our borders and countering illicit trafficking helps protect against transnational extremist threats and requires the combined efforts of US and international law enforcement agencies (LEAs), intelligence agencies, and support from DOD assets to enhance overall USG efforts.

*See JP 3-07.4,* Counterdrug Operations, *and JP 3-28,* Defense Support of Civil Authorities.

f. **Pandemic Influenza (PI) and Other Infectious Diseases.** A pandemic is an outbreak of an infectious disease that may be of natural, accidental, or deliberate origin, occurring over a wide geographic area. It is unique in that it is not a discrete event but a prolonged environment in which military operations, including any CBRN response, may continue. The National Strategy for Pandemic Influenza uses a three-pillar construct for preparation and response that can be extended to other pandemics as well. These three pillars are: EP, surveillance and detection, and response and containment. DOD plays a major role in the USG effort to contain, mitigate, and reduce the spread of PI or infectious diseases. Such actions also help preserve US combat capabilities and readiness, support USG efforts to save lives, reduce human suffering, and mitigate the spread of infection.

*See JP 3-41,* Chemical, Biological, Radiological, and Nuclear Consequence Management.

### 3. Homeland Defense Policy and Legal Considerations

a. Multiple documents provide guidance for conducting HD operations. Specific planning factors, requirements, and objectives for HD operations are contained in operation plans (OPLANs) and CONPLANs associated with the HD mission. See Appendix D, "Key Homeland Defense Legal and Policy Documents."

b. **Special Considerations.** Certain functions, such as intelligence activities, military information support operations (MISO), rules of engagement (ROE), and rules for the use of force (RUF), have specific applications and legal implications when conducted domestically.

(1) **Posse Comitatus Act (PCA).** The PCA prohibits the use of military personnel from performing various functions within the homeland. However, when directed by the President, the use of military operations for HD is a constitutional exception to the PCA. When performing HD operations, Title 10, USC, forces are not subject to the restriction of the PCA.

(2) **Intelligence Activities.** Intelligence activities refer to all activities that DOD intelligence components are authorized to undertake in accordance with (IAW) Executive Order (EO) 12333, *United States Intelligence Activities* (as amended), Department of Defense Directive (DODD) 5240.01, *DOD Intelligence Activities,* and DOD 5240.1-R, *Procedures Governing the Activities of DOD Intelligence Components that Affect United States Persons.* Intelligence activities include the collection, retention, and dissemination of intelligence by DOD intelligence components.

(a) Intelligence activities conducted by US intelligence organizations in the US and its territories are strictly controlled. Several regulations and laws specifically govern the use of DOD intelligence assets and organizations in domestic operations. The program that oversees the collection of information on US persons by the intelligence organizations is called the Intelligence Oversight Program. Its goal is to ensure that intelligence personnel do not collect, retain, or disseminate information about US persons unless done IAW specific guidelines. For intelligence purposes, a "US person" is one of the following: a US citizen; a permanent resident alien known by the intelligence agency; an unincorporated association substantially composed of US citizens or permanent resident aliens; or a corporation incorporated in the US, except for those directed and controlled by a foreign government or governments. Figure I-2 lists several policy and guidance documents for the intelligence oversight program.

## Guidance and Policy for the Intelligence Oversight Program

- Executive Order 12333 (as amended by Executive Order 13470), *United States Intelligence Activities*

- Department of Defense (DOD) Directive 5148.11, *Assistant to the Secretary of Defense for Intelligence Oversight*

- DOD Directive 5240.01, *DOD Intelligence Activities*

- DOD 5240.1-R, *Procedures Governing the Activities of DOD Intelligence Components that Affect United States Persons*

- National Geospatial-Intelligence Agency's National System for Geospatial Intelligence Manual FA 1806, *Domestic Imagery*, Revision 5, March 2009, Administrative Update: May 2011

- North American Aerospace Defense Command and United States Northern Command Instruction 14-3, *Domestic Imagery*, 5 May 2009

**Figure I-2. Guidance and Policy for the Intelligence Oversight Program**

(b) **Acquisition of Open Source Information.** Publicly available open source information can be used to obtain basic situational awareness and regional industrial knowledge on any part of the world; however, intelligence oversight still applies to information gathered on US persons or companies regardless of whether it is publicly available or not. Careful adherence to DODD 5240.01 and DOD 5240.1-R when performing such collections is critical to the success of the effort, and to avoid the appearance or conduct of questionable intelligence activities.

(c) **Acquisition of Information Concerning Persons and Organizations Not Affiliated with DOD.** Some restrictions on information gathering apply DOD wide, not just to DOD intelligence elements. IAW DODD 5200.27, *Acquisition of Information Concerning Persons and Organizations not Affiliated with the Department of Defense,* DOD policy prohibits collecting, reporting, processing, or storing information on individuals or organizations not affiliated with DOD except in those limited circumstances where such information is essential to the accomplishment of certain DOD missions outlined within the directive. DOD intelligence elements are not governed by this directive and must look to DODD 5240.01, *DOD Intelligence Activities,* and DOD 5240.1-R, *Procedures Governing the Activities of DOD Intelligence Components that Affect United States Persons,* for guidance.

*Details on intelligence support to HD can be found in JP 2-0,* Joint Intelligence.

(3) **Military Information Support Operations.** MISO are not conducted against US persons IAW law and DOD policy based on significant legal considerations. However, in addition to HD activities outside of the US homeland as part of the discussion in paragraph 5, "The Homeland Defense Operational Framework," military information support forces and equipment may also be used as part of civil authority information support elements (CAISEs) for HD and other domestic emergencies within the boundaries of the US homeland. CAISEs conduct DOD information activities under a designated LFA or civil authority to support dissemination of public or other critical information during domestic

emergencies (whether relating to national security or disaster relief operations). CAISEs are not part of any MISO program. The Joint Staff issues specific guidance for military information support forces, as well as the designated command and control (C2) authority for the mission-tailored CAISE component.

*See JP 3-13.2,* Military Information Support Operations, *for a more complete discussion on MISO.*

(4) **ROE and RUF.** US military forces must be prepared to use force. The Chairman of the Joint Chiefs of Staff Instruction (CJCSI) 3121.01B, *Standing Rules of Engagement/Standing Rules for the Use of Force for US Forces,* establishes fundamental policies and procedures that govern the actions taken by US military commanders and personnel during global DOD operations, including HD operations.

(a) ROE are directives issued by competent military authorities which delineate the circumstances and limitations under which US forces will initiate or continue combat engagement with other forces encountered. The standing rules of engagement (SROE) applies during all military operations, contingencies, and routine military functions occurring outside the US and its territories for mission accomplishment and the exercise of self-defense. **SROE does not apply to air and maritime HD missions conducted within the US and its territories or territorial seas, unless otherwise directed by SecDef. SROE do not apply to LE and security duties on DOD installations and off-installation while conducting official DOD security functions.** Supplemental ROE may be necessary to meet mission-specific ROE requirements.

*See CJCSI 3121.01,* Standing Rules of Engagement/Standing Rules for the Use of Force for US Forces, *for additional information.*

(b) RUF are directives issued to guide US forces on the use of force during various operations. The standing rules for the use of force (SRUF) apply to land HD missions occurring within US territory and to DOD forces, civilians, and contractors performing LE and security duties at all DOD installations (and off-installation, while conducting official DOD security functions),within or outside US territory, unless otherwise directed by SecDef. GCCs may augment SRUF by submitting a request for mission-specific RUF to the Chairman of the Joint Chiefs of Staff (CJCS) for SecDef approval.

(c) ROE and RUF must conform to appropriate laws including federal law (to include military law), the law of war and other relevant international laws and they must conform to the situation and locality involved. In cases where NG forces are in a state active duty status, state RUF will apply. In cases where NG forces are in a Title 32, USC, status and thus under a federally funded state control status, federal regulations may apply in addition to state law. **Commanders are responsible for the education of their personnel on ROE and RUF and their training on the use of nonlethal and lethal force.** Escalation of force, moving from nonlethal to lethal force as the situation dictates also needs to be part of the training. Self-defense is an inherent right and obligation exercised by the unit commander in response to a hostile act or demonstrated hostile intent. Individual self-defense is exercised IAW established ROE.

c. The nature of HD operations mandates consideration for employment of a variety of weapons to include nonlethal weapons and capabilities. Nonlethal capabilities may provide an effective alternative means of employing force to reduce the probability of death or serious injury to civilians or belligerents, as well as decrease the possibility for collateral damage. **Employment of nonlethal capabilities must be considered for inclusion in HD plans, ROE, and RUF.** Additionally, commanders plan and conduct rehearsals that test and exercise the adequacy of planned ROE and RUF and prepare their personnel for HD operations.

*Additional information on the employment of nonlethal capabilities can be found in DODD 3000.03,* DOD Executive Agent for Non-Lethal Weapons (NLW), and NLW Policy, *multi-Service publication Field Manual (FM) 3-22.40/Marine Corps Warfighting Publication (MCWP) 3-15.8/Navy Tactics, Techniques, and Procedures (NTTP) 3-07.3.2/Air Force Tactics, Techniques and Procedures (AFTTP) 3-2.45/US Coast Guard Publication 3-07.31,* Nonlethal Weapon—Tactical Employment of Nonlethal Weapons, *and Army Training Circular 3-19.5,* Nonlethal Weapons Training.

4. **Active, Layered Defense**

a. The *Strategy for Homeland Defense and Civil Support* calls for securing against attack through an active, layered defense. This defense strategy seamlessly integrates US capabilities in the forward regions of the world, in the geographic approaches to US territory, and within the US homeland.

b. **The Forward Regions.** In the forward regions, the objective is to detect, deter, prevent, or when necessary, defeat threats to the US. Actions may include combat operations, military engagement activities, peace operations, or preemptive measures such as direct action missions, cyberspace operations, or global strike.

c. **The Approaches.** The approaches extend from the limits of the homeland to the forward regions. The approaches are not uniformly defined, may not have boundaries, and may be characterized based on a specific situation. The primary objective of actions within the approaches is to locate threats as far from the homeland as possible and defeat them at a safe distance. The National Military Strategy (NMS) emphasizes the importance of joining the efforts of multinational partners and intragency partners to form an integrated defense. Protecting these approaches requires intelligence and when possible, enhanced, persistent surveillance that allows the US to detect, track, and if required, interdict and defeat potential threats.

d. **The Homeland.** In the event that defeating threats in forward regions and approaches fails, DOD must be postured to take immediate, decisive action to defend against and defeat the threat in the homeland. Actions in the homeland may take place simultaneously and in coordination with operations conducted in the forward regions and/or the approaches.

5. **The Homeland Defense Operational Framework**

a. The HD operational framework includes the strategies, plans, and actions taken to detect, deter, prevent, and defeat threats and aggression against the homeland. The purpose of HD is to protect against and mitigate the impact of incursions or attacks on sovereign territory, the domestic population, and critical infrastructure and key resources (CI/KR) as directed. The following are DOD HD objectives:

(1) Identify the threat.

(2) Dissuade adversaries from undertaking programs or conducting actions that could pose a threat to the US homeland.

(3) Ensure defense of the homeland and deny an adversary's access to the nation's sovereign airspace, territory, and territorial seas.

(4) Ensure access to cyberspace and information (including information systems and security).

(5) Protect the domestic population and critical infrastructure.

(6) Deter aggression and coercion by conducting global operations.

(7) Decisively defeat any attack if deterrence fails.

(8) Recovery of the military force to restore readiness and capabilities after any attack or incident.

b. The diversity of threats requires that DOD, the military instrument of national power, take a broad role to coordinate all the requirements and objectives of the HD operational framework. HD operations require integration of capabilities and synchronization of activities (i.e., arrangement of activities across time, space, and purpose) through interagency coordination, and when necessary, interorganizational coordination.

c. DOD conducts activities and operations globally intended to contribute to the defense of the homeland. They are carried out in various operational environments, including the air, land, maritime, and space domains and the information environment (which includes cyberspace). The information environment is also considered distinct, but it includes cyberspace and resides within the physical domains. HD operations are conducted IAW laws; treaties and international agreements; national authorities; and DOD, CJCS, Military Department, and Service policy and doctrine. HD operations require active and passive defenses, and DOD may conduct offensive actions (to include preemptive activities) to deter, disrupt, and destroy adversary capabilities before they can be offensively employed. Figure I-3 illustrates these relationships.

(1) Outside the US (in the forward regions and approaches), DOD conducts activities to maintain the freedom to operate in the global commons, access information, and conduct operations or campaigns to disrupt and defeat terrorists and other adversaries before they are able to execute attacks against the US homeland. DOD security cooperation activities (e.g., exercises, exchanges, experimentation), and counterproliferation and nonproliferation activities also advance working relationships and interoperability with

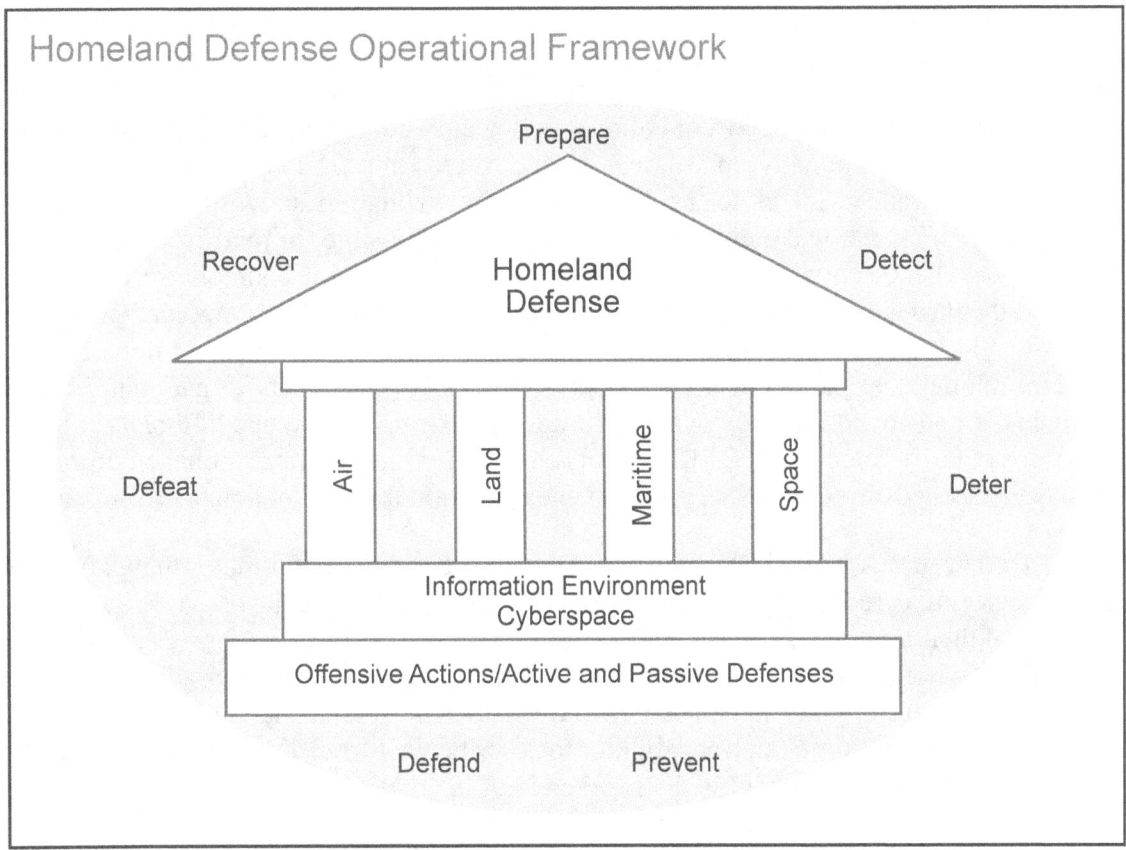

**Figure I-3. Homeland Defense Operational Framework**

friends and allies. The NG State Partnership Program (SPP) contributes to these initiatives and is part of the GCC's security cooperation program.

(2) Within the homeland, military activities are conducted in or adjacent to the land mass, airspace, and territorial waters of the US. These activities require freedom of action and full access and use of capabilities in cyberspace and space. HD includes ballistic missile defense (BMD), cruise missile defense, air interdiction, maritime interdiction, land operations, to include protection of critical infrastructure, and defensive cyberspace operations.

d. **HD operations require thorough preparation.** DOD EP activities at the strategic level may focus on actions associated with continuity of operations (COOP) and continuity of government (COG). At the operational level, however, DOD emergency preparations to defend the homeland include activities such as joint and interagency interoperability and coordination, joint training exercises and experimentation, and development of information and intelligence architectures.

e. **Early detection facilitates timely identification, tracking, and engagement decisions for threats before they reach the homeland.** In the forward regions and approaches, intelligence and when possible persistent ISR can provide decision makers with possible indications and warnings, early warning and assessments. The CONUS portion of the air domain is protected in part by NORAD's integrated tactical warning and attack assessment (ITW/AA) functions. For maritime domain awareness, the National Maritime Intelligence-Integration Office is an interagency organization that works at the national and international level to facilitate the integration of maritime information and intelligence collection and analysis in support of national policy and interagency decision makers at all levels of USG. Additionally, maritime warning utilizes mutual support agreements with other commands and agencies, to enable identification, validation, and response to threats to North America by national commands and agencies responsible for maritime defense and security. Another essential interagency organization is the National Counterterrorism Center (NCTC) that has the specific and unique mission of acquiring, integrating, analyzing, and disseminating all available USG information about terrorist threats and identities. The US and its multinational partners seek a global awareness of all threats to national security individually and collectively, to increase the ability to deal with a range of threats at home and abroad. Early detection of CBRN threats emanating from any operational environment must be integrated throughout ISR planning and execution from collection to dissemination.

f. **Deterrence is a key HD objective.** Deterrence is a state of mind brought about by the existence of a credible threat of unacceptable counteraction against adversaries, or the prospect of their missions failing to achieve desired objectives. USG offensive capabilities coupled with defensive measures and DOD EP activities may deter an adversary from threatening or attacking the homeland. The adversaries must understand USG capabilities, so the use of information-related capabilities to describe well-trained, equipped, and rapidly deployable forces conducting realistic exercises is another example of actions and capabilities that may support deterrence.

g. **DOD prevention and recovery actions for attacks on the homeland** complement those HS procedures undertaken by the public and private sectors to disrupt terrorist acts, or mitigate their effects. Recovery actions from an HD perspective are actions taken by a military force during or after operational employment to restore its combat capability and readiness.

h. **DOD must be prepared to rapidly act offensively or defensively against threats and aggression.** DOD, as directed by the President, may conduct preemptive and/or active defense actions including flexible deterrent options and flexible response options IAW international and domestic law, national policy, and directives. The objective of these operations is to destroy, degrade, disrupt, or neutralize weapons, launch platforms, support command, control, and communications, logistics, and ISR capabilities before they are employed by an adversary. Examples of offensive operations may include global strikes, direct action, and space denial. The US and its multinational partners work together to synchronize activities and measures that may include any or all of their instruments of national power.

i. **Primary HD defensive actions** include active and passive measures to defeat threats already deployed or en route to a target. Active defenses employ defensive actions (e.g., defensive counterair) and offensive actions (e.g., counterattacks) to deny a contested area or position to the enemy and are designed to reduce the effectiveness of or stop attacks on US sovereign territory, domestic population, and defense critical infrastructure (DCI). Active defenses employ land, maritime, air, space, cyberspace, and special operations forces (SOF) assets. Defenses may also include the use of information-related capabilities. The objective of HD passive defense is to reduce the probability of, and minimize the damage caused by, hostile actions. Passive defenses include force protection (FP) and critical infrastructure risk mitigation actions to reduce targeting effectiveness. They also include deception, mobility, dispersion, systems hardening and protective construction, warning and surveillance, and operations security (OPSEC).

Intentionally Blank

# CHAPTER II
## COMMAND RELATIONSHIPS AND INTERORGANIZATIONAL COORDINATION

> *"In uniform, when I talk about terrorism it's easy to assume that the war on terrorism is a military thing. It's not at all. It demands the attention and action of all [sic. instruments] of national power."*
>
> **General Richard B. Myers, US Air Force**
> **Chairman of the Joint Chiefs of Staff**
> **10 March 2004 during talks with Brazilian civilian and military leaderships**

## 1. General

a. HD is part of an active, layered defense that includes the forward regions, geographic approaches, and homeland; and is part of DOD's effort to defend in depth with domestic and international partners. The relationships of participants for some HD activities/operations may be simple, and others may be complex, but the supported joint force commander (JFC) is responsible for all participants understanding their established command and organizational relationships for the unity of command, interagency coordination, and/or interorganizational coordination required for unified action during an HD operation.

b. CCDRs exercise combatant command (command authority) (COCOM) of assigned forces, and are directly responsible to the President and SecDef for the performance of assigned missions and the preparedness of their commands. CCDRs prescribe the chain of command within their commands and designate the appropriate authority to be exercised by subordinate commanders. Dependent upon the location and type of threat to the homeland, CDRUSNORTHCOM and/or CDRUSPACOM would be designated as a supported CCDR for HD.

*For more details regarding establishment of support relationships and responsibilities of supported and supporting CCDRs, see JP 1,* Doctrine for the Armed Forces of the United States.

c. A consideration that significantly affects command relationships for HD is that virtually all the most lethal and nonlethal strategic threats to the homeland in the USNORTHCOM AOR are based in the AORs of other GCCs. This requires command relationships for a collaborative federated architecture for targeting by USNORTHCOM with the Joint Staff Intelligence Directorate, the intelligence directorates of the CCMDs, the National Joint Operations and Intelligence Center, and other supporting CCDRs; especially those supporting GCCs in whose AORs those strategic threats reside.

*For more details regarding the relationships and process for federated targeting support, see JP 3-60,* Joint Targeting.

## 2. Unified Action

a. Unified action synchronizes, coordinates, and/or integrates joint, single-Service, and multinational operations with the activities of other interagency partners, NGOs, IGOs, and the private sector to achieve unity of effort. Because of the normal multitude of interagency partners and other participants, HD is essentially a model of unified action, especially with regard to how forces and other organization can coordinate and operate in the same operational environment on a day-to-day basis.

b. In the **air domain**, Canadian forces work with US forces to provide aerospace warning concerning North America through NORAD. In the US, the US Air Force (including the Air National Guard [ANG]), the Federal Aviation Administration (FAA), and the Transportation Security Administration (TSA) are just a few of the many organizations/agencies involved.

c. In the **land domain,** during preparation for potential HD operations, specific US Army and US Marine Corps units, and the land component commands United States Army, North (USARNORTH), and United States Army, Pacific (USARPAC) coordinate and conduct exercises with DHS and other interagency partners to support HS. Army National Guard (ARNG) and Army Reserve units also work with civil authorities and interagency partners. Recent examples include border security, counterdrug (CD), and vulnerability assessments of the defense industrial base (DIB). USARNORTH also works with Canadian forces through security cooperation activities to build their capacity to conduct a cooperative defense to secure the land approaches supporting in depth defense of the homeland. Command relationships and interagency coordination required for the complex operational environment for HD are planned and routinely rehearsed in national level exercises.

d. In the **maritime domain,** the Royal Canadian Navy and Coast Guard Canada team with US Navy and United States Coast Guard (USCG) forces through cooperative training and combined exercises to ensure both nations' maritime forces and agencies are poised to respond to maritime threats to either nation. In the US, DOD has the lead for HD, but many USG departments and agencies are partners in a collaborative approach.

e. In the **space domain,** use of civilian and military space capabilities is essential to the effectiveness of conducting HD. Canadian forces work with US forces to provide aerospace warning of space and missile attack through the NORAD Agreement. The Joint Functional Component Command for Space (JFCC SPACE) at United States Strategic Command (USSTRATCOM), and the Service space forces conduct operations to protect and defend the right to operate in space and are responsible for securing DOD critical assets in space. GCCs with HD responsibilities provide FP for those ground-based space assets located in their respective AORs. USSTRATCOM and JFCC SPACE coordinate with CJCS, other CCMDs, DOD and USG agencies (e.g., Defense Information Systems Agency [DISA]), the National Aeronautics and Space Administration, commercial partners, and international agencies to integrate civil and military space assets.

f. For **cyberspace,** the open vulnerability and complex interrelationship of national and international networks demands closely coordinated action among the military and other government entities at all levels. The CCMDs joint cyberspace centers (JCCs), the Services, and USSTRATCOM's subordinate unified command, United States Cyber Command (USCYBERCOM), are the military front line of defense. The Secretary of Homeland Security has statutory primary agency responsibilities as the focal point for the security of cyberspace, and established the National Cyber Security Division (NCSD) within DHS for protecting USG, state and local governments, and public networks against cyberspace intrusions and attacks. USPACOM and USNORTHCOM, because of their HD and HS responsibilities, have coordination requirements for cyberspace operations through their JCCs with USCYBERCOM and potentially with NCSD, if that is not done through USCYBERCOM.

*For more information on operations in cyberspace see, JP 3-12,* Cyberspace Operations.

### 3. Command and Control Relationships and Responsibilities

a. Military forces will remain under the control of the established chain of command when conducting HD operations. In exceptional circumstances and IAW established DOD policies, NG forces may conduct HD activities while in state active duty status. These NG forces may subsequently transition to Title 32, USC, status upon request of the governor and approval of SecDef.

(1) **Secretary of Defense.** As the President's principal assistant in all matters related to DOD, SecDef exercises overall authority, direction, and control.

(2) **Under Secretary of Defense for Policy (USD[P]).** USD(P) is the principal staff assistant and advisor to SecDef for all matters on the formulation of national security and defense policy, integration and oversight of DOD policy, and plans to achieve national security objectives, including HD.

(3) **Assistant Secretary of Defense (Homeland Defense and Americas' Security Affairs) (ASD[HD&ASA]).** The ASD(HD&ASA), under the authority, direction, and control of the USD[P], serves as the principal civilian advisor to SecDef and the USD(P) on HD activities, DSCA, and Western Hemisphere security matters. The ASD (HD&ASA) provides overall supervision of HD activities of DOD pursuant to Title 10, USC, Section 138. These activities include but are not limited to the Defense Critical Infrastructure Program (DCIP); domestic antiterrorism (AT); the Defense Continuity Program; other HD-related activities; and alignment of HD policies and programs with DOD policies for counterterrorism (CT) and counternarcotics

(a) Preparedness to execute the national security missions of DOD pertaining to the defense of US sovereignty, territory, domestic population, and critical infrastructure.

(b) Defense Critical Infrastructure Program. (See Department of Defense Instruction [DODI] 3020.45, *Defense Critical Infrastructure Program [DCIP] Management.)*

(c) DOD domestic antiterrorism IAW DODI 2000.12, *DOD Antiterrorism (AT) Program.*

(d) DOD domestic CT activities, except those executed by SOF. (See DODD 5111.13, *Assistant Secretary of Defense for Homeland Defense and Americas' Security Affairs (ASD[HD&ASA]*.)

(e) DOD continuity-related activities, to include COOP, COG, and enduring constitutional government are managed under the Defense Continuity Programs. (See DODD 3020.26, *Department of Defense Continuity Programs.)*

(f) Policy guidance on HD-related education, training, and professional development programs.

(4) **DOD Chief Information Officer (CIO).** The DOD CIO is the principal staff assistant and advisor to SecDef on a vast array of information-related areas. HD support includes working with the Military Departments and DOD agency CIOs to determine systems vulnerabilities, to prevent information security incidents based upon the evolving threat to national security systems, and to respond to incidents when they occur.

(5) **Assistant Secretary of Defense (Reserve Affairs) (ASD[RA]).** ASD(RA) is responsible for the overall supervision of Reserve Component (RC) affairs and provides policy regarding the appropriate integration of RC forces into HD efforts.

(6) **CJCS.** As senior military advisor to the President, the National Security Council, the Homeland Security Council, and SecDef, CJCS has numerous responsibilities relating to HD and DSCA. These include: advising the President and SecDef on operational policies, responsibilities, and programs; assisting SecDef in implementing operational responses to threats or acts of terrorism; and translating SecDef guidance into strategic plans, including those which conform to resource levels projected by SecDef. CJCS also provides for the preparation and review of contingency plans which conform to policy guidance from the President and SecDef. CJCS reviews HD plans and operations for compatibility with other military plans and assists CCDRs in meeting their operational requirements. Finally, IAW established DOD policy, CJCS reviews and assesses requests from governors for NG HD activities and provide recommendations to SecDef.

(7) **Joint Chiefs of Staff (JCS).** The JCS is made up of the CJCS, the Vice CJCS, the Chiefs of Staff of the Army and Air Force, the Chief of Naval Operations, the Commandant of the Marine Corps, and the Chief of the National Guard Bureau. While the CJCS is the senior military advisor, the other members of the JCS are military advisors to the President, the National Security Council, the HS Council, and SecDef, as well. A member of the JCS (other than the CJCS) may submit to the CJCS advice or an opinion in disagreement with, or advice or an opinion in addition to, the advice presented by the CJCS to the President, the National Security Council, the HS Council, or Sec Def, which advice the CJCS must provide when providing his own. The individual members of the JCS also may provide advice when specifically requested.

(8) **Chief, National Guard Bureau.** Serves as a principal advisor to SecDef, through CJSC on matters involving non-federalized NG and on other matters as determined by SecDef. As the principal advisor to the Secretary of the Army and the Secretary of the

Air Force on NG matters, the Chief, National Guard Bureau assists the state adjutants general in supporting, synchronizing, and facilitating NG HD activities.

(9) **Governors of the States.** Governors retain C2 of all NG forces within their respective states that are executing HD activities on active duty IAW Title 32, USC, Sections 901-908. Governors coordinate with the National Guard Bureau (NGB) to facilitate NGB synchronization of state HD activity planning with the appropriate CCDRs to ensure NG funded HD activities do not conflict with ongoing federal missions.

b. **Geographic Combatant Commander Responsibilities.** The UCP establishes CCMDs' missions, responsibilities, geographic AORs, and functions. As stipulated in the UCP, the GCCs of USNORTHCOM and USPACOM have specified tasks for HD activities (these commanders are referred to subsequently in this publication as GCCs with geographic HD responsibilities). They are responsible for planning, organizing, and executing HD operations within their respective AORs. The other CCDRs support them and contribute to the protection of the US homeland either through actions within their own AORs (forward regions and approaches) or through global responsibilities assigned in the UCP.

(1) **Commander, North American Aerospace Defense Command (CDRNORAD).** By international agreement, CDRNORAD leads the bi-national command composed of Canadian and US forces. NORAD's primary missions are aerospace warning, aerospace control, and maritime warning for North America. CDRNORAD is responsible to the Canadian and USG communicating through the Chief of Defence Staff (Canada) (CDS) and CJCS, respectively. CDRUSNORTHCOM is normally designated as CDRNORAD. IAW the NORAD agreement, when CDRNORAD is a Canadian, CDRUSNORTHCOM will be designated Deputy Commander NORAD. While NORAD and USNORTHCOM have separate missions defined by separate authorities, parts of the USNORTHCOM AOR overlap with NORAD's operational area (OA) (in the NORAD Agreement this is normally referred to as an area of operations [AO]). The organizations are separate commands and neither is subordinate to the other or is a part of the other, but their operational focus runs in parallel with detecting, deterring, preventing, and defeating threats and aggression in the air approaches and airspace of North America. NORAD is supported by Canada Joint Operations Command (CJOC), USNORTHCOM, USPACOM, and United States Southern Command (USSOUTHCOM) in the conduct of missions assigned to NORAD. NORAD's maritime warning mission supports CJOC, USNORTHCOM, USPACOM, and USSOUTHCOM in their assigned missions to defend North America. NORAD warns of maritime threats to or against North America to enable identification, validation, and response by national commands and agencies responsible for maritime defense and security.

*See Appendix C, "North American Aerospace Defense Command, Missions, Organization, and Structure" for detailed information on NORAD.*

(2) **Commander, United States North Command (CDRUSNORTHCOM).** As directed by the President, CDRUSNORTHCOM is responsible for conducting military operations within the USNORTHCOM AOR utilizing forces to detect, deter, or defeat an incursion into US sovereign territory. CDRUSNORTHCOM has COCOM over Army, Air Force, and Marine Corps component commands and a support relationship with the US Navy

component. When forces are attached to the command for HD operations, the deployment order or execute order (EXORD) will normally establish command relationships. CDRUSNORTHCOM, normally designated a supported commander for HD, determines the appropriate C2 structure to employ these forces. CDRUSNORTHCOM may retain direct C2 of forces as the JFC, designate an existing joint task force (JTF) commander, or establish a new subordinate JTF. CDRUSNORTHCOM and subordinate JTF commanders will normally organize forces around a joint construct with functional component commanders. However, CDRUSNORTHCOM may conduct HD operations using any combination of subordinate JFCs and functional component, Service component, single Service task force (normally assigned to the Service component), or specific operational forces necessary to accomplish the mission. Figure II-1 provides the USNORTHCOM HD command relationships.

(3) **The National Guard.** NG forces may conduct HD activities in state active duty status in USNORTHCOM AOR as approved by SecDef.

*For additional information on C2, see JP 1,* Doctrine for the Armed Forces of the United States.

(a) **C2 for HD Land Operations in the USNORTHCOM AOR.** Land defense forces generally plan and execute HD land operations using a mix of Service assets, primarily those of the Army and Marine Corps. Operations can be conducted through Service task forces or joint forces. Force size, composition, and C2 relationships depend upon the situation and mission requirements. Commander, USARNORTH on order becomes the Joint Force Land Component Commander (JFLCC) for USNORTHCOM, and has a main command post and deployable contingency command post that can quickly become a full JTF with augmentation. USARNORTH has the mission to conduct HD operations in the land domain for USNORTHCOM, but current Army doctrine stipulates that division and corps headquarters (HQ) provide mission command for Army units conducting major combat operations, not theater Army operations. Nevertheless, the homeland is a unique theater of operations for the Army with special requirements, so USARNORTH could provide mission command for smaller scale HD operations. USARNORTH could therefore conduct theater opening and sustainment operations for all ground forces participating in an HD mission in the homeland.

(b) **C2 for HD Maritime Operations in the USNORTHCOM AOR.** Commander, US Navy North is the component commander to CDRUSNORTHCOM and may be designated as the joint force maritime component commander (JFMCC). The flag officer serving as Commander, Coast Guard Atlantic Area serves separately as Commander, Coast Guard Defense Force (CGDEFOR) East. Additionally, Commander, Coast Guard Pacific Area serves separately as Commander, CGDEFOR West. USCG forces under USCG Atlantic and Pacific area commanders may be designated under operational control (OPCON) of the JFMCC, as required. The Memorandum of Agreement (MOA) Between the Department of Defense and Department of Homeland Security for the Inclusion of the US Coast Guard in Support of Maritime Homeland Defense Missions and its annexes

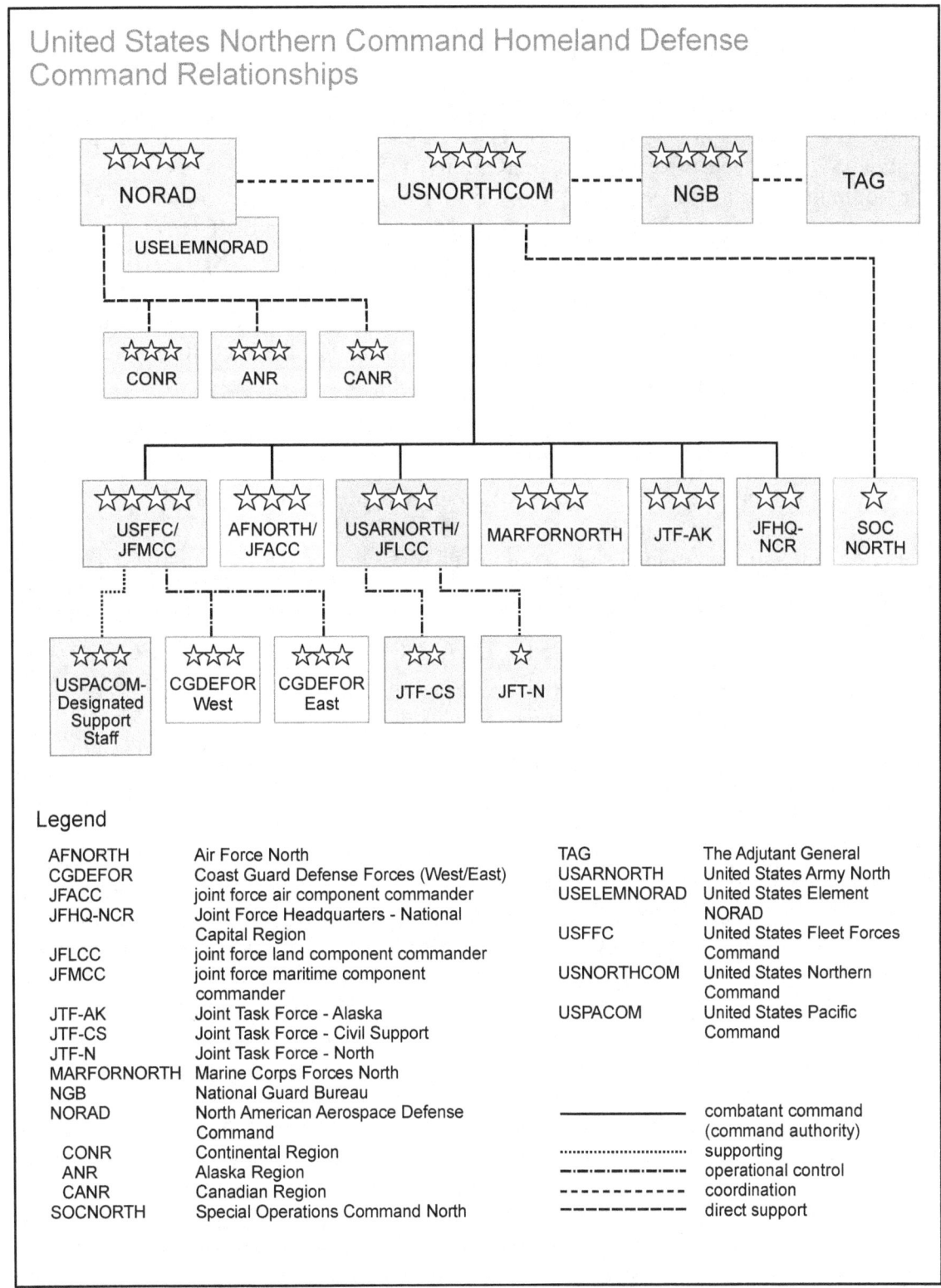

**Figure II-1.  United States Northern Command Homeland Defense Command Relationships**

provide the authority that allows USNORTHCOM, through the JFMCC, to bring all available resources to bear in conducting maritime operations within the USNORTHCOM AOR.

(c) **C2 for HD Air Operations in the USNORTHCOM AOR.** C2 for HD air operations in the USNORTHCOM AOR is complex. Where the NORAD OA and the USNORTHCOM AOR overlap, NORAD normally retains authority for the aerospace control and aerospace warning missions. The Commander, continental United States North American Aerospace Defense Command Region (CONR) is appointed the Combined Force Air Component Commander for CONUS, the Virgin Islands, and Puerto Rico. For US-only air operations within CONUS, the Commander, Air Force North (CDRAFNORTH) is designated the joint force air component commander (JFACC). CDRAFNORTH is dual-hatted as the Commander, CONR. For US-only air operations in Alaska, the Commander of the combined US-Canadian Alaskan North American Aerospace Defense Command Region (ANR) may be designated the JFACC. Close coordination between the JFACC(s) and NORAD is essential for synchronization of operations.

(d) **C2 for HD Space Operations in the USNORTHCOM AOR.** USSTRATCOM conducts space operations in direct support to USNORTHCOM's HD operations. Commander, United States Strategic Command (CDRUSSTRATCOM) has designated coordinating authority to Commander, JFCC SPACE for the planning of space operations in operational-level support of USTRATCOM's UCP missions. Commander, JFCC SPACE is responsible for the integration of military, intelligence, civil, and commercial space requirements between CDRUSSTRATCOM and CDRUSNORTHCOM. CDRUSNORTHCOM has designated CDRAFNORTH as USNORTHCOM's space coordinating authority (SCA) has primary responsibility for joint space operations planning, to include ascertaining space force enhancement requirements in support of USNORTHCOM's HD operations. CDRUSNORTHCOM or CDRUSSTRATCOM may prescribe that direct liaison is authorized (DIRLAUTH) between the SCAs to ensure prompt and timely support.

(e) **C2 for HD Cyberspace Operations in the USNORTHCOM AOR.** CDRUSNORTHCOM is responsible to defend against, mitigate, and defeat cyberspace threats against specific USNORTHCOM and NORAD systems, in coordination with USSTRATCOM and USPACOM. Finally, geographic and functional CCDRs, as well as the Services, are responsible for protecting their networks located within the USNORTHCOM AOR which are not specifically assigned or attached to USNORTHCOM.

*For more information on cyberspace operations, see JP 3-12,* Cyberspace Operations.

(f) **C2 for HD Special Operations (SO) in the USNORTHCOM AOR.** Commander, United States Special Operations Command (CDRUSSOCOM) is responsible for synchronizing planning for global operations against terrorist networks, and will do so in coordination with other CCMDs, the Services, and, as directed, appropriate USG departments and agencies. CDRUSSOCOM normally has COCOM over SOF in the US. When directed, CDRUSSOCOM relinquishes OPCON/tactical control (TACON) of US-based SOF, and OPCON/TACON is assumed by CDRUSNORTHCOM for HD operations in the USNORTHCOM AOR. Under certain circumstances, regardless of AOR, CDRUSSOCOM will exercise OPCON of SOF conducting operations in support of overseas contingencies operations. Operation orders and EXORDs should carefully delineate C2 arrangements for SOF.

(g) **Joint Force Headquarters–National Capital Region (JFHQ-NCR).** JFHQ-NCR plans, coordinates, maintains situational awareness, and as directed, employs forces for HD and DSCA in the National Capital Region (NCR) joint operations area (JOA) to safeguard the Nation's capital, excluding air defense and air warning. NORAD executes air defense operations within the USNORTHCOM AOR, to include the NCR, through the National Capital Region integrated air defense system (NCR-IADS).

(h) **Joint Task Force–Alaska (JTF-AK).** Commander, JTF-AK is assigned responsibility for HD and DSCA operations within the assigned JTF-AK JOA by CDRUSNORTHCOM. JTF-AK normally requires staff augmentation from the USNORTHCOM staff and Service components for HD and DSCA operations. The Commander, JTF-AK is also Commander, Alaskan Command (ALCOM), which is a subunified command under USPACOM.

(i) **Joint Task Force-North (JTF-N).** JTF-N supports drug LEAs in the conduct of CD and counternarcoterrorism operations in the USNORTHCOM AOR to disrupt TCOs and deter their freedom of action in order to protect the homeland. JTF-N is OPCON to USARNORTH.

(j) **Joint Task Force-Civil Support (JTF-CS).** JTF-CS is assigned to USNORTHCOM and is under OPCON of Commander, United States Army, North (CDRUSARNORTH). JTF-CS plans and integrates DOD support to the designated LFA for CBRN response utilizing five core capabilities: identification and detection; technical and nontechnical search and extraction; mass casualty and non-casualty decontamination; medical triage and stabilization; and medical and nonmedical air and ground evacuation. When approved by SecDef and directed by CDRUSNORTHCOM, JTF-CS deploys to the CBRN incident site and executes timely and effective C2 of designated DOD CBRN response forces, supporting civil authorities to save lives, prevent injury, and provide temporary critical life support. Although primarily designed for chemical, biological, radiological, and nuclear consequence management (CBRN CM), JTF-CS provides C2 for DSCA for natural disasters that may not involve CBRN response (e.g., Hurricane SANDY in 2012).

(k) **USNORTHCOM Contingency Joint Task Force(s).** When combat forces for a joint HD operation are attached to USNORTHCOM, CDRUSNORTHCOM exercises command authority delegated by SecDef as necessary to accomplish required missions or tasks. Based upon the scope and objectives of the operation, the CDRUSNORTHCOM may decide to establish one or more subordinate JTFs. For example, JTF-AK and JTF-NCR, when activated, could have combat forces attached to conduct HD operations within their respective JOAs. For various HD contingencies, CDRUSNORTHCOM may task component command or supporting commanders to provide the core of a new JTF HQ with augmentation from the other Service components.

(4) **Commander, United States Pacific Command.** CDRUSPACOM integrates and synchronizes a broad range of military activities to defend the homeland against attacks and aggression. These activities include the protection of the domestic population and the critical infrastructure of the US and its territories and the domestic population and critical

infrastructure of the sovereign nations, commonly called freely associated states, under the Compact of Free Association in the USPACOM AOR: Federated States of Micronesia, the Republic of the Marshall Islands, and the Republic of Palau. The US territories located in the Pacific and the nations included in the Compact of Free Association include: American Samoa, Northern Mariana Islands, Guam, Baker, Howland, and Jarvis Islands, Johnston Atoll, Kingman Reef, Midway Atoll, Palmyra Atoll, Wake Atoll, the Federated States of Micronesia, the Republic of the Marshall Islands, and the Republic of Palau. USPACOM also contributes to the active, layered defense in-depth of the western approaches to CONUS and Alaska. CDRUSPACOM is the supported commander for HD within the USPACOM AOR. Support relationships are coordinated among CCDRs with geographic HD responsibilities such as against threats from outside the AOR (e.g., USPACOM supporting USNORTHCOM). CDRUSPACOM may be tasked to support the collaborative federated architecture for targeting required by CDRUSNORTHCOM.

(a) **C2 for HD Land Operations in the USPACOM AOR.** The Commanding General (CG), United States Army Pacific (USARPAC) assumes functional component commander responsibilities as the land component commander for the USPACOM portion of the US and its territories. CG USARPAC is dual-hatted as the Commander Joint Task Force-Homeland Defense (JTF-HD) and is responsible for providing situational awareness of the JTF-HD JOA (including CBRN CM and DSCA) and for working closely with applicable federal, state, tribal, and local agencies when orchestrating DOD operations. All HD activities are coordinated with USNORTHCOM, USSTRATCOM, and others across AOR boundaries, including those concerning Hawaii and Alaska.

(b) **C2 for HD Maritime Operations in the USPACOM AOR.** The Commander, United States Pacific Fleet (COMUSPACFLT) conducts maritime homeland defense (MHD) operations in the USPACOM AOR, supports CDRUSNORTHCOM in the conduct of MHD operations in the USNORTHCOM AOR, and supports the USCG for maritime homeland security (MHS). COMUSPACFLT conducts MHD operations with assigned forces within the USNORTHCOM AOR in close coordination with USNORTHCOM's JFMCC while keeping CDRUSPACOM informed. In addition, COMUSPACFLT coordinates maritime operations with Commander, Coast Guard Pacific Area, who serves separately as CGDEFOR West. USCG forces under USCG Pacific area commanders may be designated either OPCON or TACON to COMUSPACFLT as required. The Memorandum of Agreement Between the Department of Defense and the Department of Homeland Security for Inclusion of the US Coast Guard in Support of Maritime Homeland Defense and its annexes provide the authority that allows USPACOM, through COMUSPACFLT, to effectively bring all available resources to bear in conducting maritime operations within the USPACOM AOR.

(c) **C2 for HD Joint Air Operations in the USPACOM AOR.** The Commander, Pacific Air Forces (COMPACAF) is the theater JFACC for the USPACOM AOR and maintains a theater joint air operations center in Hawaii.

*See JP 3-30,* Command and Control for Joint Air Operations, *for details regarding theater JFACC, joint air operations center, and C2 for joint air operations.*

(d) **C2 for HD Space Operations in the USPACOM AOR.** USSTRATCOM conducts space operations in direct support to USPACOM's HD operations. CDRUSSTRATCOM has designated JFCC SPACE as USSTRATCOM's SCA responsible for the deconfliction, prioritization, and integration of military, intelligence, civil, and commercial space requirements between CDRUSSTRATCOM and CDRUSPACOM. CDRUSPACOM has designated COMPACAF as USPACOM's SCA with primary responsibility for joint space operations planning, to include ascertaining space force enhancement requirements in support of USPACOM's HD operations. CDRUSPACOM or CDRUSSTRATCOM may authorize DIRLAUTH between the SCAs to ensure prompt and timely support.

(e) **C2 for HD Cyberspace Operations in the USPACOM AOR.** CDRUSPACOM is responsible for protection of USPACOM networks in the USPACOM AOR. HQ USPACOM will coordinate cyberspace operations with USPACOM component commands, subordinate unified commands, JTFs, direct reporting units and other CCMDs through the USPACOM JCC. CDRUSSTRATCOM, through its USCYBERCOM, is the supporting commander for cyberspace operations within the USPACOM AOR. USCYBERCOM normally provides a cyberspace support element (CSE) to USPACOM for major exercises and operations to support cyberspace operations and as required for liaison between USCYBERCOM and USPACOM components. For HD, USPACOM and USCYBERCOM have coordination requirements with DHS through its NCSD as primary agency for protecting USG and public networks against cyberspace intrusions and attacks. Functional CCDRs and the Services are responsible for protection of their networks located within the USPACOM AOR, but not assigned or attached to USPACOM.

(f) **C2 for HD SO in the USPACOM AOR.** SO conducted in the USPACOM AOR are normally under the COCOM of CDRUSPACOM while OPCON is exercised through the theater Special Operations Command, Pacific (SOCPAC). In the USPACOM AOR, SOCPAC conducts theater special operations command (TSOC) functions and serves as the USPACOM entry point for all SOF matters. SOCPAC is tasked to conduct regional activities that may support future operations.

(g) The Commander, JTF-HD employs two task forces and subordinate coordination teams in two Pacific OAs associated with Task Force Hawaii and Task Force Guam. These forces, along with local installations, conduct HD operations and respond to support requests from civil authorities.

(h) To assist the Commander, JTF-HD in accomplishing HD missions, organizations such as the USPACOM Joint Intelligence Operations Center, Joint Interagency Task Force West, SOCPAC, and USPACOM Service components provide intelligence, staff augmentation, interagency coordination, and military forces as necessary. All USPACOM Service and functional components involved in HD operations provide situational awareness and coordinate their actions with JTF-HD, per USPACOM CONPLAN 5002 Homeland Defense.

(5) **Commander, United States Southern Command (CDRUSSOUTHCOM).** CDRUSSOUTHCOM is responsible for providing contingency planning, operations, and

security cooperation for Central and South America, the Caribbean (except US commonwealths and territories and foreign nations and territories within the USNORTHCOM AOR), and Cuba, as well as for the FP of US military resources within these locations. CDRUSSOUTHCOM is also responsible for defense of the Panama Canal and canal area. Key contributions to defending the homeland are to:

(a) Provide interdiction of air and maritime threats to the homeland before they enter the USNORTHCOM AOR, and provide C2 military handoff when/as appropriate.

(b) Provide designated lead CCDR element within Joint Interagency Task Force–South (JIATF-S). JIATF-S works with partner nations and US LEAs to stem illegal production and trafficking of drugs, which undermine security of nations in the USSOUTHCOM and USNORTHCOM AORs and threaten overall US national security. USSOUTHCOM's role provides significant insight into extant and emerging threats to the homeland. This includes contacts established during JIATF-S missions that may be determined by USSOUTHCOM or USNORTHCOM, to be an HD threat.

(6) **Commander, United States European Command (CDRUSEUCOM), Commander, United States Africa Command (CDRUSAFRICOM) and Commander, United States Central Command (CDRUSCENTCOM).** CDRUSEUCOM, CDRUSAFRICOM and CDRUSCENTCOM play vital roles in defending the homeland and supporting CDRUSNORTHCOM and CDRUSPACOM for HD. Specifically, they provide a forward presence to obtain information on potential adversaries that may be planning attacks on the homeland, and they can deny adversaries freedom of access to the air, land, and maritime approaches to the homeland. CDRUSEUCOM and CDRUSCENTCOM may be tasked to support the collaborative federated architecture for targeting required by CDRUSNORTHCOM.

c. **Functional CCDR Responsibilities**

(1) **Commander, US Strategic Command.** CDRUSSTRATCOM is the lead CCDR for strategic deterrence planning and is responsible for executing strategic deterrence operations as directed. Specifically, CDRUSSTRATCOM conducts the following activities associated with defending the homeland:

(a) Synchronize planning for global missile defense and coordinate global missile defense operations support. Provide missile warning information to CCDRs and allies, and provide assessment of missile attack if the appropriate CCMD is unable to do so. Advocate for missile defense and missile warning capabilities. Provide alternate global missile defense execution capability as directed, and as required to ensure COOP.

(b) Plan, coordinate, and execute lethal (nuclear and conventional) and nonlethal global strike, as directed.

(c) Support the collaborative federated architecture for targeting required by CDRUSNORTHCOM for HD.

(d) Synchronize planning for cyberspace operations, to include direction of DOD information network (DODIN) operations and defense to secure, operate, and defend DOD networks, and to defend US critical cyberspace assets, systems, and functions. Directs DODIN operations and defense in coordination with CJCS and CCMDs. Coordinate with other CCMDs and appropriate USG departments and agencies prior to the generation of cyberspace effects that cross AORs in response to cyberspace threats.

<u>1</u>. USCYBERCOM, as the USSTRATCOM subordinate unified command for cyberspace operations, plans, coordinates, integrates, synchronizes, and conducts activities for offensive and defensive cyberspace operations and defense of DODIN; and when directed, conducts cyberspace operations to enable actions in the physical domains, facilitates freedom of action in cyberspace, and denies the same to adversaries. USCYBERCOM can support HD cyberspace operations in collaboration with USNORTHCOM, USPACOM, and DHS, by coordinating activities within the required AOR and assisting with expertise and capabilities directed and made available.

<u>2</u>. USCYBERCOM normally provides CSEs to GCCs to support cyberspace operations during major operations and exercises, and for liaison between the GCCs' components and USCYBERCOM Service components, as required.

*For details regarding USCYBERCOM and all aspects of cyberspace operations, see JP 3-12,* Cyberspace Operations.

(e) Planning, integrating, and coordinating ISR in support of strategic and global operations, as directed. The Director, Defense Intelligence Agency (DIA) is dual-hatted as the Commander, Joint Functional Component Command for Intelligence, Surveillance, and Reconnaissance (JFCC ISR) and fulfills the ISR as the Joint Functional Manager for ISR and associated processing, exploitation, and dissemination systems capabilities. CDRUSSTRATCOM established JFCC ISR to develop allocation recommendations for ISR and associated processing, exploitation, and dissemination capabilities while supporting oversight and management of the ISR enterprise by developing and synchronizing operational ISR plans and allocation strategies to integrate national and theater capabilities to satisfy the CCDRs' requirements.

(f) Synchronizing planning for DOD countering weapons of mass destruction (CWMD) efforts. This effort is coordinated through the United States Strategic Command Center for Combating Weapons of Mass Destruction (SCC-WMD), which is integrated with the Defense Threat Reduction Agency (DTRA). The SCC-WMD is a subordinate command to USSTRATCOM and integrates and synchronizes DOD-wide efforts in support of the CWMD mission by planning, advocating and advising CCMDs on WMD-related matters to include doctrine, organization, training, materiel, leadership, education, personnel, and facilities.

(2) **Commander, United States Special Operations Command.** CDRUSSOCOM leads, plans, synchronizes, and as directed, executes global operations against terrorist networks. US Special Operations Command also organizes, trains, equips, and deploys combat ready SOF in support of other CCMDs. For operations conducted in the

homeland, CDRUSSOCOM serves as either a supported or supporting commander for selected CT activities and serves as a supporting commander to the GCCs with geographic HD responsibilities within their respective AORs. Theater objectives are established by GCCs based on national objectives, and are an integral part of a theater campaign plan. The integration of SOF through the TSOC can help the commander attain these objectives.

(3) **Commander, United States Transportation Command.** CDRUSTRANSCOM provides common-user and commercial air, land, and sea transportation, terminal management, and aerial refueling to supported commanders. For HD operations, CDRUSTRANSCOM provides, upon request, a director of mobility forces to advise on air mobility support operations.

d. **Reserve Component Responsibilities.** The RC of the US Armed Forces consists of the ARNG, the Army Reserve, the Navy Reserve, the Marine Corps Reserve, the ANG, the Air Force Reserve and the Coast Guard Reserve. By virtue of their geographic dispersion throughout the US, the RC represents a significant military response capability for HD missions and activities.

(1) **National Guard.** The NG is established in all 50 states, the territories of Guam, Puerto Rico and the Virgin Islands, as well as the District of Columbia. The NG has both state and federal missions, protecting life and property during times of emergency under the authority of the state governors, and acting as reserves of the Army and the Air Force during wartime. The NG thus serves in both federal and state-controlled duty statuses. The NG is commanded by the state or territory governors when under state or territory control, with the exception of the District of Columbia NG, for which the President is Commander in Chief. Federal missions of the NG conducted under state control include training activities related to readiness requirements established by the Departments of the Army and Air Force, DSCA missions, and conducted pursuant to Title 32, USC. State missions are conducted in state active duty status IAW state law. When federalized pursuant to Title 10, USC, National Guard units and personnel are subject to federal C2. Governors may employ the NG for the HD mission in state active duty status or as provided in Title 32, USC, Section 902, for activity such as critical infrastructure protection (CIP.)

*For more detailed information regarding the NG and Homeland Defense, see DODD 3160.01,* Homeland Defense Activities Conducted by the National Guard.

(a) **NGB.** NGB is a joint activity of DOD and serves as the channel of communications for all matters pertaining to the NG between the Departments of the Army and Air Force, the 50 states, District of Columbia, Commonwealth of Puerto Rico, Guam, and the US Virgin Islands. The Chief, National Guard Bureau, is the principal advisor to the SecDef, through the CJCS, on matters involving non-federalized NG forces, and on NG matters to the Secretaries of the Army and Air Force and to the Service Chiefs of the Army and Air Force. The NGB participates with the Army and Air Force staffs in the development and coordination of programs pertaining to or affecting the NG. The NGB formulates and administers the programs for the training, development, and maintenance of the ARNG and ANG.

(b) **The Adjutants General (TAGs).** Governors normally exercise C2 over their state NG through their TAGs. The TAGs are responsible for maintaining trained and equipped ARNG and ANG forces able to respond to both state needs and federal requirements pursuant to the policies of and as resourced by the Secretaries of the Army and the Air Force. The TAGs, through their NG joint force HQ-state (NG JFHQ-State), provide expertise and situational awareness to DOD to facilitate integration of federal and state-level activities and promote unity of effort in domestic responses; develop plans, coordinated with appropriate authorities, that augment, support, or perform assigned or authorized federal missions; provide operational information for domestic operations, through NGB; participates in federal domestic preparedness planning, training, and exercises; and develop plans to support civil authorities in response to man-made or natural disasters.

(2) Reserves. The reserves, with the exception of the Coast Guard Reserve, at all times are subject to a federal chain of command pursuant to Title 10, USC, as defined by their parent Services.

(a) The Coast Guard Reserve serves in a federal duty status, but can function subject to the authority of two federal departments. The Coast Guard is organized under DHS during peacetime, its activities governed primarily by Title 14, USC. When federalized pursuant to Title 10, USC, Coast Guard units and personnel are administered by the Department of the Navy within DOD.

(b) Title 10, USC, Section 12304, was amended in 2011 (National Defense Authorization Act of 2012) to allow the rapid mobilization of Army, Navy, Marine Corps, and Air Force reserves for domestic incident response, subject to policies established by the Office of the Secretary of Defense and their parent Services.

*For additional information on the RC mobilization/demobilization process, see JP 4-05,* Joint Mobilization Planning.

e. **CCDRs HD Relationships.** Synchronization is the arrangement of military actions in time, space, and purpose to produce maximum relative combat power at a decisive place and time. Integration should include military and civilian organizations as appropriate. The JFC must be fully cognizant of the strategic direction in order to establish the priorities, timelines, goals and objectives for HD missions that allow synchronization and integration of all operations for unified action. Federal and international law, international and command agreements, DOD policies, and selected OPLANs provide guidance which the CCDR must integrate to achieve synchronization. Command arrangement agreements (CAAs) establish procedures and delineate responsibilities between two or more CCDRs concerning mutual support, interface, and cooperation. They prescribe the arrangement necessary to support the employment of forces from one CCDR to another and the control of these forces operating within a specific AOR or JOA. CAAs may also delineate information and intelligence dissemination requirements in order to enhance coordination for planning and execution of cross-AOR operations. CAAs must remain consistent with DOD guidance as promulgated from SecDef and CJCS. The CAA between CDRUSNORTHCOM and CDRUSPACOM establishes the methodology under which transfer of forces between the two

CCMDs is executed in support of HD missions. Processes, C2 arrangements, and communication requirements are representative items addressed in the document.

*For further information on CAAs as governing directives, refer to JP-1,* Doctrine for the Armed Forces of the US.

## 4. Interagency Coordination

a. **Interagency Coordination and Interoperability.** During a HD operation, civil authorities continue to operate and perform many of their respective routine functions. HS activities of some interagency partners may overlap with some HD activities, and while the major military activities that are the responsibilities of DOD cannot be accomplished by other interagency partners, their support is essential. Unity of effort among all HD participants is fundamental and essential. HD operations are conducted in a complex operational environment that contains thousands of different jurisdictions (federal, state, tribal, and local), many agencies and organizations, and several allies and multinational partners. From a USG perspective, this necessitates coordinated and integrated activities, that have been previously exercised/rehearsed to facilitate effective interagency interoperability in addition to unity of effort. The inherent interrelationships between HS, HD, and DSCA, and the potential for transition between those missions, creates a dynamic and complex environment in which interagency coordination and resulting interoperability could prove critical. From a DOD perspective, properly understanding and executing the multiple command relationships and organizational relationships required for simultaneous execution of HS, HD, and DSCA will require the utmost in interagency coordination.

(1) Within the US homeland and its approaches, forces may face continuous media scrutiny. Personnel need to be sensitive to jurisdictional considerations, and should also be mindful of political dimensions of a domestic response, yet should be quick to respond to deal with the varied threats to the homeland.

(2) Interagency coordination is conducted at the strategic, operational, and tactical levels to address multiple topics, to include HD. At the strategic level, DOD interaction takes place through the National Security Council (NSC), the senior interagency forum for consideration of policy issues affecting national security. The NSC is chaired by the President and its regular attendees (both statutory and non-statutory) are the Vice President, the Secretary of State, the Secretary of the Treasury, SecDef, and the Assistant to the President for National Security Affairs. The CJCS is the statutory military advisor to the NSC. Along with its subordinate committees, the NSC is the principal means for coordinating executive departments and agencies input in the development and implementation of national security policy.

(a) The **National Security Council Principals Committee (NSC/PC)** is the senior interagency forum for consideration of national security policy issues. It meets at the call of the National Security Advisor, in consultation with the members of the NSC/PC.

(b) The **National Security Council Deputies Committee (NSC/DC)** serves as the senior sub-Cabinet interagency forum for consideration of policy issues affecting national security and includes as its regular members, the Deputy Secretary of State, the Deputy Secretary of Defense or USD(P), the Vice CJCS, and Deputy National Security Advisor (who serves as chair). Members generally review and monitor the work of the NSC interagency process (including interagency policy committees [IPCs] as they are established). The NSC/DC provides day-to-day crisis management and reports to the NSC.

(c) The **NSC IPCs** work the development and implementation of national security policies by multiple departments and agencies of the USG. They are the main forum for interagency coordination of national security policy and replace the previous system of policy coordination committees. These IPCs can include those associated with maritime security, aviation security, and border and transportation security. Additionally, the CT security group, attended by the Joint Staff and appropriate Office of the SecDef representatives, provides an operationally focused forum to coordinate USG activities associated with global terrorist threats.

(3) CCDRs, with appropriate SecDef and CJCS direction, approval, and coordination, may interact with and provide input to select NSC entities regarding significant national and/or theater level issues on which a commander can present unique insight and value-added recommendations.

(4) Operational coordination is conducted within appropriate joint force command centers and their corresponding non-DOD counterparts. It is not complete until it includes interagency planning considerations, which are intrinsic rather than optional in the planning process. CDRUSNORTHCOM and/or CDRUSPACOM may seek approval and guidance from SecDef to conduct interagency planning and coordination when appropriate.

(5) Each CCDR has the prerogative to organize or tailor the interagency coordination function differently based on mission requirements. Regardless of the title of the interagency coordination effort, it should include agency representatives, command liaison officers (LNOs), and staff representatives who collaborate to share information, and analyze ongoing activities, actions, implications, and/or consequences, and participate in planning; interagency coordination efforts should ensure that the commander and staff are completely informed on interagency issues and implications.

*For more information on interagency coordination, see the discussion on joint interagency coordination group in JP 3-08,* Interorganizational Coordination During Joint Operations.

(6) Information sharing is critical to the efficient pursuit of unity of effort. A proven approach to information sharing during interorganizational coordination is the use of transparency to develop shared situational awareness of common objectives. Commanders and interagency partners should provide guidance on what information needs to be shared with whom and when. DOD information should be appropriately secured, shared, and made available throughout the information life cycle to appropriate mission partners to the maximum extent allowed by US laws and DOD policy. Critical to transparency of information sharing is the proper classification of intelligence and information.

b. **Navy and Coast Guard Arrangements.** Legal sensitivities and limited LE authority on the part of DOD forces require special consideration when conducting MHD missions. Such missions require flexibility, time-critical response, and immediate access to a broad spectrum of capabilities and associated forces. Success is based upon DOD/DHS relationships and operational C2 constructs. The USCG remains at all times a military service and branch of the armed forces with specialized LE authority (Title 14, USC). The USCG resides within DHS and only transfers to the Department of the Navy upon declaration of war or when the President so directs. USCG is therefore required to maintain a state of readiness to function as a specialized service within the Navy in time of war. MHD missions often require a similar approach to conducting MHS operations. As a result, agreements exist between DOD and DHS to permit flexible support to both mission areas with regard to US Navy and USCG efforts.

(1) **Maritime Homeland Defense Missions.** CCDRs are tasked to take all appropriate actions to identify, and as required, intercept, maritime threats as far as possible from the US and its territories. This necessitates coordinating DOD operations with interagency partners and international partners, as required, as part of the whole-of-government response to threats to the homeland. To assure success, the USCG works cooperatively with the Navy during peacetime and assists DOD in performance of any activities for which the USCG is especially qualified. In the event a GCC requires USCG resources to support a specific long-term operation, DOD submits a request for forces (RFF) to DHS. For most MHD missions, expeditious transfer of forces is necessary and C2 structures exist to facilitate such transfers between the US Navy and USCG. C2 authority to execute such missions is effective when directed in the initiating directive or appropriate order.

(2) **Maritime Homeland Security Missions.** The USCG has the predominant role in MHS and exercises its LE authorities in waters subject to US jurisdiction and on the high seas. It provides an armed deterrent and response to acts of terrorism in the maritime domain. The USCG may exercise TACON over the capabilities or the forces of agencies, to include the DOD, which supports with LE missions. DOD forces operating under USCG TACON remain under DOD command. Such DOD forces may not participate directly in the seizure, arrest or other similar activities unless the law otherwise authorizes such participation and SecDef approves of the specific activity. DOD personnel are authorized to operate and maintain equipment to support federal LEAs IAW US law and applicable DODD. Such assistance includes enforcing CD, immigration, and custom laws as well as conducting foreign and domestic CT operations. For example, DOD capabilities may be used to intercept maritime threats in order to permit USCG to conduct boarding and inspection operations, even to the point of warning shots and disabling fire. Most MHS support operations by DOD are of short-duration based on USCG Commandant or area commanders' requests. CCDRs and USCG area commanders periodically plan, train, and exercise appropriate MHS missions. As with equivalent MHD missions, the supporting force for MHS missions generally provides such support on a non-reimbursable basis when such activities provide equivalent training or operational benefit to DOD maritime forces.

c. **Maritime Operational Threat Response Process**

(1)  The National Strategy for Maritime Security (NSMS) and the MOTR Plan are directed in the National Security Presidential Directive (NSPD)-41/Homeland Security Presidential Directive (HSPD)-13, Maritime Security Policy.  The MOTR Plan operationalizes NSPD-41/HSPD-13 and the NSMS by outlining a coordinated USG response to a vast array of threats in the maritime domain, to include nation-state military threats, piracy, state/non-state criminal, unlawful, or hostile acts such as smuggling; and threat vessels with cargo and/or personnel which require investigation and disposition.  At the tactical level, the MOTR process exists to achieve a USG desired outcome and to coordinate and assist in bringing additional capabilities to bear on a threat.

(2)  The MOTR plan pre-designates USG departments and agencies with lead responsibilities, clarifies interagency roles and responsibilities, and establishes protocols and procedures that are utilized for a coordinated response to achieve the USG's desired outcome regarding a particular threat.  The MOTR pre-designated leads are developed using the following criteria:  USG desired outcome; agency authorities; agency capabilities; agency asset availability; magnitude of the threat; and existing law.

(3)  The MOTR protocols and procedures allow rapid response to short-notice threats and require interagency partners to begin coordination activities at the earliest possible opportunity when one of the following triggers are met:

(a)  Any specific terrorist or state threat exists and USG department and agency response action is or could be imminent.

(b)  More than one USG department or agency has become substantially involved in responding to the threat.

(c)  The USG department or agency lacks the capability, capacity, or jurisdiction to address the threat.

(d)  Upon resolving the threat, the initial responding USG department or agency would not be able (or authorized) to resolve the disposition of cargo, people, or vessels acting under its own authority.

(e)  The threat poses a potential adverse effect on the foreign affairs of the US.

(4)  The MOTR coordination process is conducted through a virtual network of interagency national and operational command centers and is coordinated by the Global MOTR Coordination Center.  This coordination process is the key element in determining which agency will lead the USG response and what other agencies will be needed to support the response effort.  Additionally, the MOTR protocols include a process for transitioning the lead from one agency to another.

(5)  Successful MOTR execution relies on the operations-intelligence linkage enhanced by ongoing efforts to achieve maritime domain awareness and to facilitate timely decision making.  The goal is to identify threats as early and as distant from the homeland as

possible, but no later than the time required to defeat or otherwise overcome threats at a safe distance from the US. This is enabled by maintaining an understanding of the effects of the global maritime domain on the security, safety, and economy of the US.

*For additional information on maritime domain awareness, refer to JP 3-32,* Command and Control for Joint Maritime Operations.

   d. **Land Domain Operational Threat Response Process**

   (1) The homeland is a unique theater of operations for US ground forces and is subject to special requirements. The US Army and US Marine Corps components to USNORTHCOM and USPACOM work with DHS, other interagency partners, and civil authorities to support HS, which complements some aspects of HD. The US Army and USARNORTH also support security cooperation activities with North American partners to help build a cooperative military defense as part of the effort to secure the land approaches and ensure defense of the homeland in depth.

   (2) Many of the missions and activities that are conducted in the land domain in phase 0 support other interagency partners and civil authorities, such as defense support of LEAs, CD, CWMD, countering TCOs, FP, security cooperation activities with Mexico and the Bahamas, and partnership with Canada. These efforts contribute to and are enablers to both HS and HD. Those efforts help constitute the prevent aspect of HD.

*For additional information on the joint land domain, refer to JP 3-31,* Command and Control for Joint Land Operations.

   e. **Aviation Operational Threat Response Process**

   (1) An AOTR ensures a comprehensive and coordinated USG response to air threats against the US or its interests. NSPD-47/HSPD-16, Aviation Security Policy, prescribes the AOTR Plan as part of the overall national aviation policy. Simply stated, the AOTR is primarily to counter asymmetric threats involving civilian aviation, but includes considerations for interagency coordination to defend against foreign military air and missile attacks. Several DOD HD responsibilities in the air domain fall within the protocols of the AOTR. DOD response capabilities remain an integral part of the overall national response in this domain in support of HD and HS complementary goals and missions.

   (2) AOTR comprises immediate actions, generally short duration in nature, to counter the full range of airborne and ground-based aviation security threats. These threats include, but are not limited to: attacks using civilian aviation (i.e., commercial/general aviation) aircraft as weapons against ground-based targets; attacks against aircraft, including hijacking and air piracy; attacks using standoff weapons, including man-portable air defense systems; attacks involving civilian aircraft carrying WMD; and attacks against aviation transportation system infrastructure. AOTR execution begins when intelligence or other information is received that an incident is imminent or occurring and that an immediate response is necessary and concludes when the threat has been defeated or otherwise resolved.

(3) DOD shall, upon AOTR execution and, time permitting, initiate secure communications with appropriate agencies to facilitate the timely flow of information. This will allow for appropriate consultation related to the initial DOD airborne operational response, as well as coordination of related LE actions or other security measures. DOD performs the following activities specific to AOTR, as appropriate:

(a) Specific Airborne Threats (an ongoing or potential attack from the air domain):

1. Through CCDRs and NORAD, SecDef directs the necessary supporting measures to facilitate effective airborne response and to mitigate subsequent effects of an ongoing or potential attack from the air domain. In extreme circumstances this includes a determination made in consultation with the Department of Transportation (DOT) and DHS, whether to implement emergency security control of air traffic measures. Unless the President directs otherwise, DOD is the only USG department authorized to direct engagement using deadly force against airborne civilian aircraft that present an imminent threat to the US or US interests.

2. Interdiction of designated flights of interest that do not present an immediate threat to the US or its interests, as deemed necessary by SecDef or designee. This includes response to a threat against aircraft with US persons onboard that occurs overseas, in coordination with DOS and the affected countries, as appropriate.

3. Conducting air defense against airborne hostile military threats.

(b) General Threats:

1. Conducting air defense against threats to DOD assets and infrastructure on DOD installations.

2. Response to other aviation threats globally, including airborne or ground-based actions taken at the request of foreign partners, and when directed by SecDef or the President.

*For more information on the full range of air operations, refer to JP 3-01,* Countering Air and Missile Threats; *and JP 3-30,* Command and Control for Joint Air Operations. *For more information on the AOTR, refer to the* Aviation Operational Threat Response Plan, *March 26, 2007.*

## 5. Interorganizational Coordination Considerations

a. The threat is better recognized as existing across a continuum that ranges from nation states down to individuals and small groups, who are intending on doing harm to the US. Today, HD mission response forces involve multiple organizations. Operation NOBLE EAGLE (ONE), the NORAD, USNORTHCOM, and USPACOM operation aimed at defending the homeland, involves active duty personnel from the United States Air Force (USAF), United States Navy (USN), the Canadian Forces, and/or NG members federalized for the mission. These military forces coordinate with DOT (FAA), DHS, DOJ and with other federal agencies as appropriate. A response to a possible hijack situation would involve the private sector as well as local first responders. For example, airline companies, private or municipal airports, local municipalities, and other non-federal entities will be responsible for the aircraft and any airports where the aircraft may attempt to land or be directed to land. This demonstrates the complex environment in which DOD forces must respond to certain threats that involve multiple jurisdictions (federal, state territorial, local, and tribal) with domestic partners and international/multinational partners (e.g., NORAD).

b. The HD C2 structure will depend upon early identification of the responsibilities, authorities and capabilities of USG organizations which support HD, plus the additional considerations of other governmental or nongovernmental organizations, and multinational forces. The resulting complexity of C2, mission planning, and operational execution should drive early identification of the desired end states and necessary collaboration with the operational partners. Moreover, the JFC with HD missions should also account for likely media scrutiny and sovereignty and jurisdictional issues. For example, MHD operations may transition from HD to HS to DSCA missions or vice versa with the selection of the primary agency being dependent upon both the developing real-time situation and the USG desired end state. HD and DSCA operations can occur simultaneously or transition from one to another. Therefore, HD missions in the homeland and in the approaches many times are truly dynamic as situations may change in minutes or hours versus days or weeks.

*For additional information on interorganizational coordination with regard to HD, refer to JP 3-08,* Interorganizational Coordination During Joint Operations.

**6. Multinational Forces**

To conduct the full range of HD operations, CCDRs should consider all instruments of national power—**military, diplomatic, economic, and informational,** as well as multinational and nonmilitary organizations. When a response force resides within an alliance, the procedures and structure of that alliance will normally determine the operational level leadership. When a response force is based in a coalition (or a lead nation structure in an alliance), the designated lead nation will normally select the operational level leadership. While the President and SecDef retain command authority over US forces, it is often prudent or advantageous to place appropriate US forces under the TACON of a foreign commander to achieve specified military objectives for reasons such as maximizing military effectiveness and ensuring unity of effort.

a. **Theater Security Cooperation (TSC) Efforts.** The US seeks the cooperation of numerous foreign governments and multinational forces and other international partners to achieve its national security goals, to include defense of the homeland. CCDRs plan and conduct security cooperation activities to encourage and enable countries to work with the US to achieve strategic objectives. Strengthening security relations with multinational partners increases their capabilities to contend with common challenges.

(1) In the forward regions, CCDRs and their components conduct security cooperation activities with partner nations that help provide the outer layer of HD.

(2) GCCs with geographic HD responsibilities have AORs with very different characteristics. In addition to its vast airspace, the USPACOM AOR is predominantly maritime and includes considerable political, religious, cultural, social, and economic diversity. It encompasses the Asia-Pacific region, with numerous sovereign nations and one-half of the Earth's surface. The area includes five of seven US security treaty allies, extensive international waters covered by international law, as well as US territories under US law, treaties, or compacts. The USNORTHCOM AOR is primarily continental, with extensive land borders and coastal regions. It includes Canada, Mexico, The Bahamas, Turks and Caicos Islands, Bermuda, the British Virgin Islands, Puerto Rico, the US Virgin Islands, and the US (excluding Hawaii and Pacific territories) with multiple legal and policy concerns. USNORTHCOM TSC efforts with Canada and Mexico directly impact US defense in depth in the land domain which is unique to this AOR.

(a) **Engaging and Shaping.** Security cooperation enhances access, readiness, and training by strengthening partnerships and regional security. This will involve specific focus areas as described in the Guidance for Employment of the Force (GEF). GCCs with geographic HD responsibilities address commander's communication synchronization in their security cooperation planning efforts. CCDRs seek to diminish the conditions that terrorists exploit and to support activities that deny sanctuary to terrorist actors. The plans also strengthen and improve collaboration between joint commands, agencies at all levels of government, and regional partners.

(b) **Enabling Continental Defense.** Cooperative defense in association with US regional partners enhances successful continental defense, achieving mutual security interests and the desired HS and HD shaping objectives. TSC activities are essential to both USNORTHCOM support of HS and the HD mission through mutually beneficial partnerships. Military and civilian interoperability and cooperation begins by establishing and maintaining relationships, which then build to include combined education, training, engagement, equipping, and exercises supported by intelligence and information sharing, exchange of LNOs, and other activities that facilitate HD. Cooperative defense helps foster appropriate relationships to leverage complementary capabilities and capitalize on limited resources. Finally, current efforts toward an integrated North American defense warrants an increase in HD exercises and personnel exchanges.

(3) Various initiatives and agreements exist that forge relationships and provide for multinational coordination in the defense of the homeland. For example, the recently signed Canada-United States Combined Defense Plan (CANUS CDP) is another step towards an integrated North American Defense.

b. **Alliance Support to HD.** Various alliances may be a source additional of HD support. For example, Article 5 of the North Atlantic Treaty states: "an armed attack against one or more of them in Europe or North America shall be considered an attack against them all and consequently they agree that, if such an armed attack occurs, each of them, in exercise of the right of individual or collective self-defence..." When the US was attacked on 11 September 2001 the North Atlantic Treaty Organization invoked Article 5 and provided NATO Airborne Warning and Control System to help patrol US airspace and initiated Operation ACTIVE ENDEAVOUR as part of a AT effort.

c. **Other Multinational Considerations.** Many activities can increase US partners' capabilities and create the conditions for establishing new multinational partnerships to contend with mutual challenges. The GEF outlines a series of security activities that a CCDR can use to advance long-term security cooperation goals and objectives with multinational partners wherever feasible and mutually supportive. These activities include:

(1) Multinational exercises, training, education, and experimentation.

(2) Counternarcotics assistance.

(3) Countering WMD activities.

(4) Defense and military contacts.

(5) Defense support to public diplomacy (e.g., developing information programs in regional languages that complement other security cooperation activities).

(6) Security assistance.

(7) Other programs and activities (e.g., Regional Defense Counterterrorism Fellowship Program, and Defense Environmental International Cooperation).

(8) NG SPP.

d. The operational environment and the coordinated and integrated action of all contributors may blur the distinct contribution of any individual organization or capability in isolation from all others. This is particularly true when contemplating the complex environment within the homeland. Each organization has unique capabilities that may not be easily duplicated by other departments, agencies, or organizations. The supported JFC should continually address the challenge of coordinating, integrating, and synchronizing the wide range of available capabilities to defend the homeland. Employment of nonlethal capabilities should be considered in any situation requiring direct fire capabilities.

e. To achieve the objectives, unified action, and the synchronization and integration of military operations in time, space, and purpose, the JFC must consider many factors, to include:

(1) What objectives, when achieved, will attain the desired end state?

(2) What sequence of actions is most likely to achieve the objectives?

(3) How can the resources of the joint force and interagency and multinational partners be applied to accomplish that sequence of actions?

(4) What is the likely cost or risk to the joint force in performing that sequence of actions?

*For additional information on multinational coordination, see JP 3-16, Multinational Operations.*

# CHAPTER III
## PLANNING AND OPERATIONS FOR HOMELAND DEFENSE

*"I am telling you all, this is the defense mission of the next century–homeland defense, fair and simple. It will take several different forms. Protection against terrorist attacks using chemical or biological weapons. Protection against attacks, cyber[space] attacks from people using computers to bring down air traffic control systems or utility systems or whatever. And homeland defense against world errant nations using a ballistic missile or two. So homeland defense is the mission of the next century."*

**The Honorable John J. Hamre**
**Deputy Secretary of Defense (1998)**
**3 February 1998 at a speech given to the Adjutant Generals Association**
**of the United States**

## 1. General

The threat to the homeland is both difficult to predict and increasingly diverse. The likelihood of conventional large-scale land attack on the US may be remote; however, the wide-range of threats that do exist must be addressed. In modern times, US forces have concentrated on defeating threats as far away from the homeland as possible and that remains the overarching goal. The central idea is to protect the homeland from external threats and aggression using integrated strategic, operational, and tactical offensive and defensive measures as necessary. The ability to detect, deter, prevent, or, if necessary, defeat threats is a required capability to protect the homeland. Specific planning factors, requirements, and objectives for HD operations are contained in OPLANs and CONPLANs associated with the mission. An additional list of documents is included in Appendix D, "Key Homeland Defense Legal and Policy Documents."

## 2. Operational Environment Factors

a. **Civil and Military Relationships.** Civil-military relationships may be more complicated during HD operations because the military operations will be taking place in our homeland. Regardless of the size and scope of the particular operations, inevitably they will involve multiple jurisdictions (such as cities, counties, regions, tribes, and states). As a result, multiple agencies and organizations will participate, some of which may directly or indirectly support military operations and some of which may conflict with them, not because of different loyalties, but because of different authorities. Managing such relationships will require significant time and effort on the part of federal, state, local, and tribal authorities to ensure proper coordination. Interagency forums, associations, information sharing, and constant communications will be vital enablers. Interagency coordination and synchronization with the number of governmental and nongovernmental entities may assume a level of importance not matched in most overseas theaters of operations.

b. **Communications Synchronization and Public Affairs (PA)**

(1) The JFC's communications synchronization should support the broader USG effort and closely coordinate and solicit support from other agencies and organizations. This should be commander-driven, proactive, and synchronized with respect to all themes, messages, images, and actions.

(2) **Public Affairs.** The role of PA in HD operations is to support the JFC by communicating truthful and factual unclassified information about DOD activities to US, allied, national, international, and internal audiences. Due to the involvement of other USG departments and agencies in HD missions, military PA will operate in an interagency environment which requires cooperation, coordination, and unity of effort. The goal of PA in HD operations is to enable all USG departments and agencies to speak with one voice and provide consistent, factual information to the public. As the federal agency with lead responsibility for HD, DOD develops key messages and provides PA guidance. Supporting agencies conduct their respective PA operations in concert with this guidance. PA should be included in all phases of planning and coordination from the onset of HD operations. Specific DOD PA responsibilities are outlined in various CCMD plans and standing PA guidance. The EXORD for the incident will provide the PA posture and media engagement policy. Incident specific guidance will be developed by the primary agency in coordination with participating agencies.

*For more information on PA, see JP 3-61, Public Affairs.*

c. **Non-DOD Federal, State, Territorial, Local, and Tribal Planning Factors**

(1) Interorganizational coordination must occur between elements of DOD and non-DOD federal, state, local, and tribal agencies as well as other engaged USG departments and agencies for the purpose of achieving HD objectives. Positive and active participation by command interagency staff members from the interagency coordination office, group, or planning cell can be used to mutual benefit.

(2) Commanders and their staffs should consider the interrelationship between HD and DSCA operations (i.e., the potential for transition between the missions and simultaneous operations).

d. **Strategic Guidance**

(1) General military planning guidance and strategy are provided in high-level policy documents such as the Defense Strategic Guidance and the NMS. Specific planning factors, requirements, and objectives for HD operations are contained in OPLANs and CONPLANs associated with the mission. An additional list of documents is included in Appendix D, "Key Homeland Defense Legal and Policy Documents."

(2) **Legal Considerations.** Military operations inside the homeland can present unique and complex legal issues. Certain military functions, such as intelligence operations,

ROE, and RUF, have specific applications and legal implications when conducted domestically. Staff judge advocate legal advice should be as early in the operation planning process as possible.

## 3. Intelligence Sharing for Homeland Defense

a. The success of interagency coordination or interorganizational coordination, as the case may be, for unified action in HD operations hinges upon timely and accurate information and intelligence. Information sharing facilitates intelligence and information sharing environments that should include as many essential participants as possible, understanding that not all are capable of participating in a collaborative environment. When possible, a collaborative intelligence sharing environment should be capable of generating and moving intelligence, operational information, and orders where needed in the shortest possible time. Intelligence staff responsibilities can be found in the JP 2-0 Series. Coordination for information sharing, and especially intelligence sharing, should begin early in all HD planning processes.

b. The architecture which supports this type of environment needs to be dynamic, flexible, and capable of providing multinational partners and interagency participants' rapid access to appropriate data. It should facilitate the capability of the IC to focus on supporting the JFC and subordinate joint force components and to integrate support from and to non-DOD agencies and NGOs as needed.

c. The intelligence sharing architecture is configured to provide the baseline data needed to support commanders at all levels. CCDRs are responsible for the intelligence sharing architecture for their commands and all assigned, attached, and supporting elements. For contingency operations, subordinate JFCs, supported by their intelligence directorates, are responsible for establishing the intelligence architecture required to accomplish the HD mission. In HD, it is particularly important that effective fusion of intelligence, CI, LE information, and other available threat information occurs. This will assist in developing a more accurate assessment of threats to the homeland and may prevent strategic or tactical surprise.

d. The parameters under which DOD operates are different in the US than they are overseas. In the past, one individual typically dealt with foreign information and the other domestic. Today both now involve elements of foreign and domestic information. Determining the nature of the data required and the right units to gather it are areas that often require judge advocate input regarding the legal authorities for information gathering. Intelligence activities in the homeland are strictly governed by the Constitution, applicable laws, the policies and procedures authorized in DODD 5240.01, *DOD Intelligence Activities*, and other relevant DOD policies (Intelligence Oversight). These policies permit DOD intelligence missions in the homeland if the subject of the intelligence effort is definitively linked to defense-related foreign intelligence and counterintelligence (CI) activities. Intelligence oversight policies also provide established guidance and requirements and perform activities or missions other than intelligence activities using domestic imagery, such as incident assessment and awareness. However, intelligence oversight policies also provide specific guidance and regulations to ensure or safeguard against unauthorized collection against US persons (citizens, legal residents and organizations). Special emphasis shall be given to the protection of the Constitutional and privacy rights of US persons.

e. LE information received by DOD frequently contains US person information. US person definition, or information concerning persons and organizations not affiliated with DOD is subject to various statutory and regulatory rules and processes. Military criminal investigation organizations' agents or the Federal Bureau of Investigation (FBI) may provide sensitive threat information derived from ongoing LE or CI investigations. It is imperative that DOD personnel handling LE information be fully cognizant of all restrictions and processes for receipt, retention, handling, dissemination, and oversight of US person and other LE information.

## 4. Joint Fires

Joint fires are fires delivered during the employment of forces from two or more components in coordinated action to produce desired effects in support of a common objective. Joint fires may be provided to assist air, land, maritime, or SO forces in conducting HD activities within an operational environment framed by complex legal limitations and significant interagency coordination. Although major operations against a major adversarial power remain highly unlikely, various strategic and tactical threats require capabilities and preparations to deter or defeat them. For that reason, the supported JFCs for HD have plans/orders for HD operations that anticipate the use of joint fires across the range of military operations. The following preparations provide useful examples of the challenges of employing joint fires in HD.

a. **Deterrence and Preemptive Self-Defense.** The complexity and diversity of the strategic threats to the homeland range from intercontinental ballistic missiles (ICBMs) to terrorists with WMD. The common factor is that such attacks would have a devastating effect of strategic proportions. From a joint fires perspective, HD strategy provides US counterforce capabilities that have a deterrent effect that minimizes the threat of an overt attack of strategic proportion by a major adversarial power. For threats from some rogue state and non-state actors, a deterrence strategy may not work, so an active layered defense in depth complements the deterrence capabilities. Also, the use of joint fires to include global strike options in preemptive self defense is a strategic consideration.

(1) The threat of ballistic missile attack against the homeland is the one strategic threat by a rogue state that would require the use of fires to protect the homeland. The limited defense option for BMD was developed as part of the BMD strategy, and will be discussed under Paragraph 6, "Protection."

(2) Operation NOBLE EAGLE. While initially conceived in the immediate aftermath of the 11 September 2001 attacks, this operation incorporates both the response to terrorist use of aircraft as weapons and NORAD's air defense mission. ONE and air defense will be discussed under Paragraph 6, "Protection."

(3) Terrorist threats to the homeland from overseas may require use of joint fires through military CT operations, or in support of LE activities. Terrorist threats within the homeland are a HS mission rather than a matter of HD, unless directed otherwise by the President.

b. **Maritime Joint Fires.** Maritime joint fires provide significant capabilities against any maritime based threat to the homeland. The protections provided in the sea approaches and maritime domain support HS and HD to include use of fires when necessary. Maritime forces can be employed to rapidly destroy, intercept, or neutralize conventional and terrorist threats both at sea and ashore given actionable intelligence. These assets are used to keep potential threats at bay far from US shores, but could be deployed close to home if threats dictate. Both lethal and nonlethal fires are options. The maritime aspect of air and missile defenses will be discussed under Paragraph 6, "Protection."

(1) A variety of maritime threats to the homeland exists and may include cargo ships, fishing boats, semi-submersibles and military vessels. Once a vessel has been identified as a threat to the homeland, surface warfare options may be employed to detect, deter, prevent, and defeat the delivery of the weapons, cargo, or people to the intended target(s). Naval forces may take action as defined by the chain of command, the SROE and supplementary measures, if any.

(2) Depending on the threat, maritime HD options may be determined through the MOTR plan protocol process. Within the USNORTHCOM AOR, the JFMCC directs maritime HD operations that may include appropriate Service forces, USCG, or SOF to detect, deter, prevent, and defeat threat vessels.

c. **Land Based Fires.** The HD environment presents complex operational challenges for joint fires due to the necessity to achieve unity of effort within an operational environment of sovereign states (with NG units), and the need to interface with a number of disparate government agencies, NGOs, and the private sector. Land based fires for HD operations require significant coordination among the partnerships of federal, state, territorial, tribal, and local governments and agencies, especially since there is a significant overlap between DOD executing HD and LE organizations executing HS and supporting HD. Land based fires for air and missile defenses are discussed under Paragraph 6, "Protection."

d. **Supporting Fires.** Conducting HD US-only air missions may require a high degree of dynamic targeting that relies on rapid coordination and integration of assessment, surveillance, and attack assets in real-time. In the homeland environment, it is likely that dynamic targeting and deliberate targeting (via air tasking orders [ATOs]) would require close coordination and integration with FAA operations.

*See JP 3-30,* Command and Control for Joint Air Operations, *for information on coordinating and executing ATOs, and JP 3-60,* Joint Targeting, *for information on dynamic targeting.*

e. **Cyberspace Operations.** The HD environment also presents unique challenges for the JFC in the selection and engagement of targets in cyberspace. Because specific attribution of cyberspace threats and their geographic location are often difficult to determine, the JFC must abide by the ROE.

**5. Movement and Maneuver in the Conduct of Homeland Defense**

a. **Land Operations in the Conduct of Homeland Defense**

(1) The GCCs with geographic HD responsibilities should anticipate, plan, and be prepared for land offensive and defensive operations. Large scale HD operations involving maneuver forces, combined arms maneuver and the conduct of major combat offensive or defensive operations would be an extraordinary circumstance involving extraordinary decisions by the President of the US. However, these types of operations are planned and prepared for within the doctrinal realm of HD. HD land defense actions may include: movement and maneuver within the land, sea, or air domains; decisive fires (lethal and nonlethal); closing with and destroying a determined enemy; sustaining a joint force; and setting conditions for a return to peace. Specific HD land operations in support of HD may include security operations through FP tasks or protection of critical infrastructure. Defensive land operations will make use of existing USG departments' and agencies' capabilities where possible (e.g., DHS).

(2) Land operations in the conduct of HD are planned and executed by the GCCs, through their respective CCMDs and their subordinate commands, either Service-specific task force HQ or JTFs. Commanders consider the scope of the operational environment, the specified and implied tasks, and span of control when selecting the appropriate C2 relationship. In addition, commanders should consider: the interagency environment; the effect of current operations on the civilian populace; and the role of the state, tribal, and local LEAs, when executing HD operations. Based upon available forces, each GCC with geographic HD responsibilities has identified subordinate commands that establish or source HQ for HD operations.

(3) Although land defense forces may be required to defend in the short term, decisive results require shifting to the offense as soon as possible. However, HD operations should be of limited duration and should conclude when the land forces achieve the objectives of the operation.

(4) **US Northern Command Land Operations**

(a) CDRUSNORTHCOM may employ designated land component response forces from the Army and Marine Corps to detect, deter, prevent, and defeat threats or aggression within the AOR. USARNORTH is a Service component command that has also been designated by the CDRUSNORTHCOM as the standing joint force land component command. USARNORTH could also be designated by CDRUSNORTHCOM as a JFC and provide C2 of subordinate JTFs and land forces for HD and DSCA missions. USPACOM provides a quick reaction force (QRF) and rapid response force (RRF) for HD operations in the Alaska JOA. USNORTHCOM also has QRF and RRF packages available for HD operations. In addition, individual states possess NG quick reaction forces that may be used in response to a HD situation.

1. Figure III-1 shows how land forces may be requested, provided, and employed to respond to a crisis requiring a rapid response. When directed by the President or SecDef to conduct HD operations, CDRUSNORTHCOM can consider several initial land force options, as part of the joint effort: employ a QRF or RRF; employ a JTF with OPCON over a QRF or RRF; employ a JFLCC with OPCON over a QRF or RRF; or employ USARNORTH as a single-Service HQ with OPCON of a QRF or RRF. Based on this decision, the CDRUSNORTHCOM sends a RFF to the Joint Staff. Once the RFF is approved, force providers are directed to source personnel and equipment through Service components and provide them to CDRUSNORTHCOM. If a larger force is required, then follow-on forces can be employed. These follow-on forces may combine with the QRF or RRF as a task force, under a JTF. A dedicated QRF/RRF would only be utilized in a very small or isolated incident requiring quick reaction.

2. United States Army Forces North. The Army component command of USNORTHCOM, CDRUSARNORTH has been designated to serve as the JFLCC for USNORTHCOM, including QRF/RRF missions. CDRUSARNORTH plans and prepares for potential HD operations through continuous coordination with other Service components, the NGB, NG JFHQ-State, Title 32, USC, JTFs, and federal, state, local, and tribal agencies. USARNORTH designated task forces/JTFs can provide C2 for Title 10, USC, forces designated to conduct HD missions.

3. United States Marine Corps Forces, North (USMARFORNORTH). In addition to command responsibilities, USMARFORNORTH supports, coordinates, and provides advice to CDRUSNORTHCOM on the employment of Marine forces when they are attached to USNORTHCOM for the conduct of HD operations.

(b) Although considered extraordinary, conditions may arise that require conventional land operations within the continental limits of the US (to include Alaska). In such instances forces will be made available to USNORTHCOM. These operations will be guided by established doctrine, principles and fundamentals. Procedures for identifying C2 structures, requesting and employing response forces, and coordinating actions will be consistent with established doctrine. Special considerations will likely apply due to the unique nature of operating in the homeland environment and the requirement for DOD-wide and interagency coordination. Figure III-2 illustrates the HD land operations sustained process. Conventional land forces are provided to CDRUSNORTHCOM per the RFF process described above, and allocated to the JFLCC or the commander, joint task force (CJTF) who will have OPCON over these forces.

*For more information, refer to USNORTHCOM CONPLAN 3400, Homeland Defense.*

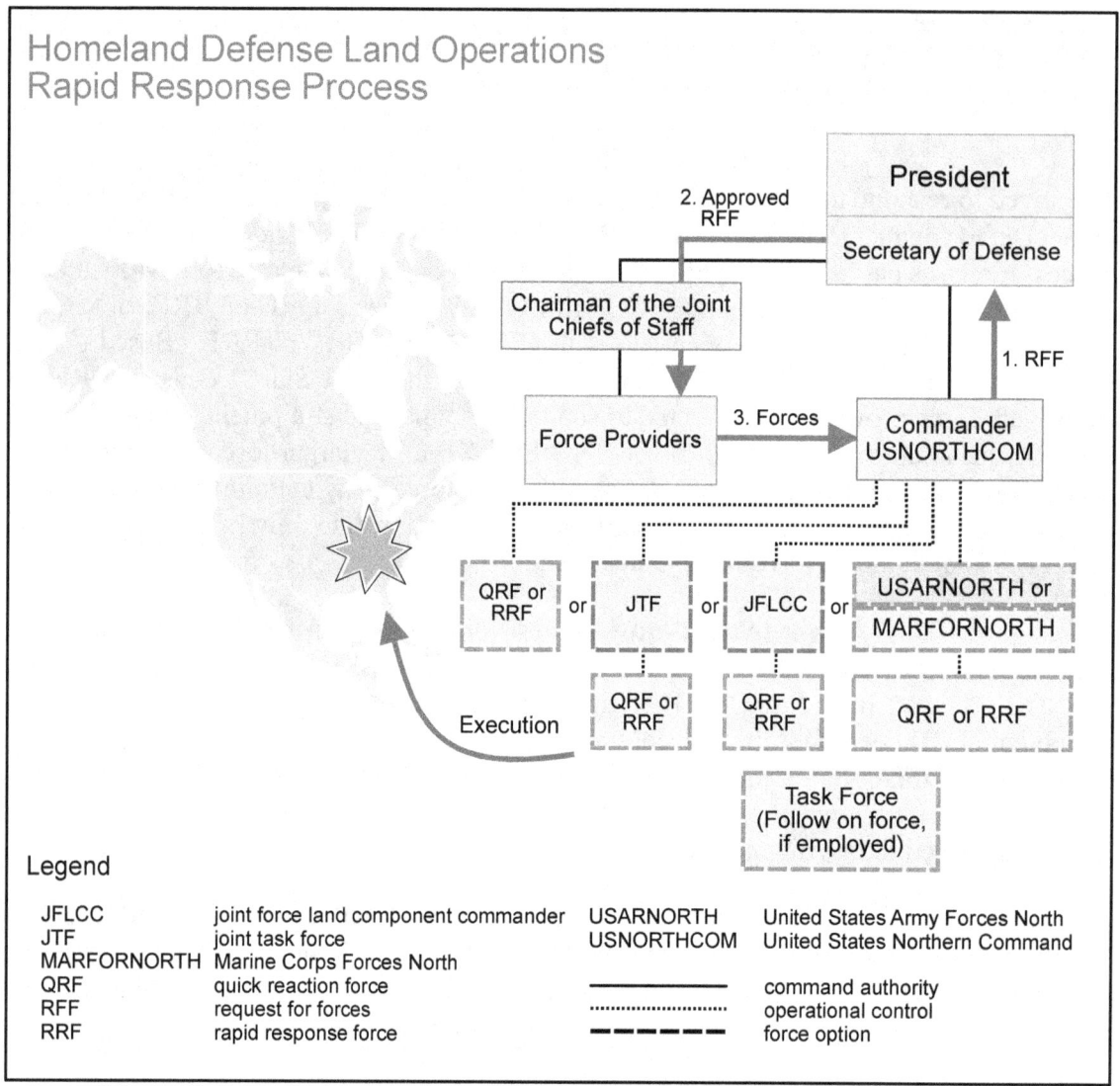

**Figure III-1. Homeland Defense Land Operations Rapid Response Process**

(5) **US Pacific Command Land Operations**

(a) CDRUSPACOM established JTF-HD as the HQ responsible for land HD operations on all bases and in all US territories within the USPACOM AOR. CG, USARPAC is dual hatted as the Commander, JTF-HD. Commander, JTF-HD provides trained and ready forces in support of security operations, from engagement to warfighting. These forces promote regional stability and provide crisis response.

(b) Commander, JTF-HD has two task force structures to respond to HD/DSCA requirements. Task Force-Hawaii is a scalable command, depending on the scope of the response as determined by USARPAC. Commander, Joint Region Marianas is designated Commander, Task Force-Guam under Commander, JTF-HD. For land operations, and in coordination with civil authorities, these units are assigned the following tasks:

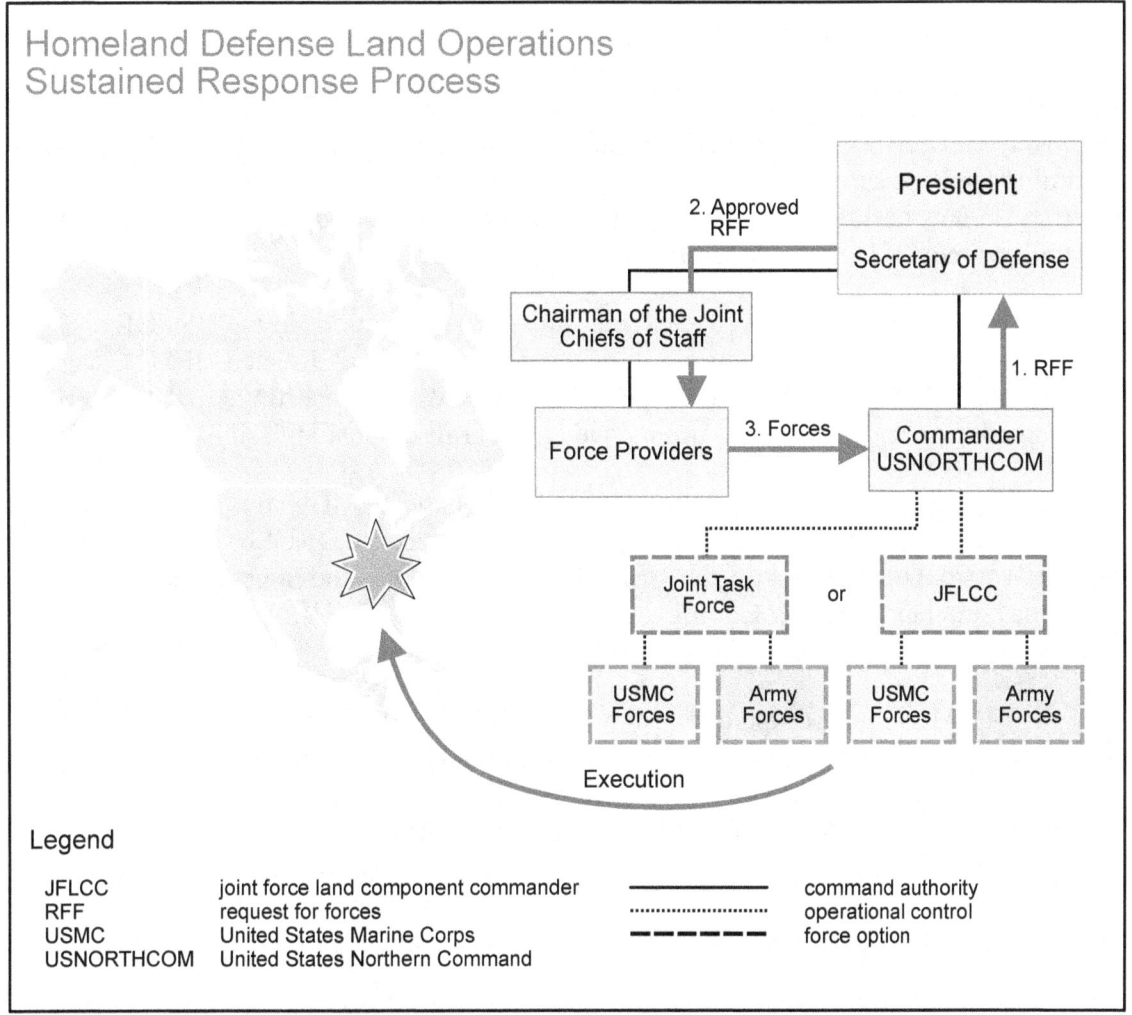

**Figure III-2. Homeland Defense Land Operations Sustained Response Process**

1. Detect, deter, prevent, and defeat attacks within their assigned OA.

2. Plan and conduct deterrence operations.

3. Defeat threats within the assigned OA.

4. Employ forces to protect military installations and assigned DCI, national critical infrastructure, and the critical infrastructure of the sovereign nations of the freely associated states.

*For more information, refer to USPACOM CONPLAN 5002,* Homeland Defense.

b. **Maritime Operations in the Conduct of Homeland Defense.** The conduct of maritime HD is the responsibility of the cognizant GCC: CDRUSNORTHCOM for CONUS and Alaska, Puerto Rico and US Virgin Islands; and CDRUSPACOM for Hawaii, the Pacific US territories, and the Freely Associated States located in the Pacific AOR. When directed by the President, responsibility for harbor defense, harbor approach defense, and sea control in the US littoral is shared between the USN and the USCG.

(1) Maritime operations in support of HD offer distinct challenges due to the nature of execution in or near the homeland in conjunction with the interagency partners. DOD is the LFA for MHD per the MOTR plan. Through the relevant CCDR, DOD provides an active, layered defense and responds to maritime threats to the homeland. MOTR decisions regarding lead and supporting agency roles for each particular maritime event are based on existing US law, desired USG outcome, greatest potential magnitude of the threat, response capabilities required, asset availability, and authority to act.

(2) The JFMCC plans and executes maritime operations in the USNORTHCOM AOR while supporting the operations of the other components as directed. JFMCC can plan and execute distinct USNORTHCOM MHD missions while supporting NORAD maritime warning mission and aerospace warning and control (air defense) missions when required.

(3) COMUSPACFLT, when designated as the JFMCC for CDRUSPACOM, conducts MHD operations in the USPACOM AOR, supports CDRUSNORTHCOM in the conduct of MHD operations in the USNORTHCOM AOR, and supports the USCG for maritime homeland security. Coordination between CCDRs for HD is addressed in specific CAAs.

(4) Maritime HD operations may be accomplished independently or in support of other operations. When established, a maritime AO can include international and territorial waters, harbor approaches, ports, waterfront facilities, and those internal waters and rivers that provide access to port facilities (including associated airspace). The JFMCC plans and conducts HD operations to: maintain sea control; strengthen port security and harbor defense and countermining operations; ensure strategic mobility; provide a secure environment for US and coalition forces; and support other component commanders, as directed.

*For further information see JP 3-32,* Command and Control for Joint Maritime Operations. *For additional discussion of Navy C2 and commander, task force integrated air and missile defense, see also Navy Warfare Publication (NWP) 3-32,* Maritime Operations at the Operational Level of War, *and NTTP 3-32.1,* Maritime Operations Center. *For further information on the maritime composite warfare commander, see NWP 3-56,* Composite Warfare Doctrine. *For more information, refer to USNORTHCOM CONPLAN 3400,* Homeland Defense.

### (5) **Countermining and Mine Countermeasures (MCM) Operations**

(a) Mining of homeland waters by enemies can be conducted by a variety of methods from surface vessels, air, submarines, or swimmers and/or divers. The objective of countermining is to prevent mining. Detection of mining activity is a priority for maritime surveillance systems monitoring the seaward approaches and internal waterways. Under the 2002 Maritime Transportation Security Act, the USCG is the LFA for maritime homeland security to include the prevention and detection of mining within waters subject to US jurisdiction. MCM operations can be conducted for the following reasons:

<u>1</u>. Bottom mapping for operational environment awareness prior to an event.

<u>2.</u> Exploratory operations to identify suspected mine threat and/or boundary of the threat area.

<u>3.</u> Clearance operations to locate, identify, and neutralize mine threats.

(b) Maritime forces may support MCM operations by providing protection for MCM assets and providing logistics support for ashore staging areas in the AO. Maritime forces provide air and surface patrol craft to enforce a security zone which encompasses the MCM OA in order to protect MCM forces from harassment or attack. Logistics support to MCM forces is limited to messing, berthing, and potable water supplies. In the event that logistics support is required, consideration should be given to basing MCM assets with or adjacent to maritime forces to economize security and logistics support.

*For further information, see JP 3-15,* Barriers, Obstacles, and Mine Warfare for Joint Operations.

(6) **Sea Lines of Communications and Chokepoint Operations.** Seaward security is a focused maritime operation that complements broader maritime operations designed to maintain sea lines of communications. The primary objective is to provide for the safe passage of strategic sealift and commerce to and from deep water and to deny use of these areas to enemy forces. Similarly, maritime forces can be employed in a chokepoint (e.g., narrow strait or canal) to provide for the safe passage of friendly forces through that chokepoint. Maritime units can be employed as part of a force—air, surface, and submarine units and their supporting systems, positioned across the likely courses of expected enemy transit—for early detection and rapid warning, blocking, and destruction of the enemy.

(7) **Maritime Interception Operations (MIO), Expanded Maritime Interception Operations (EMIO), and Boarding**

(a) MIO are designed to halt the movement of designated items into or out of a nation or area. Units involved in MIO not only provide unit presence, but may also use reasonable force if a vessel is noncompliant, subject to applicable ROE. MIO vary from one to the next. The specific political, geographic, and tactical factors and the legal authority on which the MIO are based influence the enforcement procedures.

(b) MIO are a USN core mission. Many USN ships are capable of conducting compliant and certain types of noncompliant boardings. Maritime forces may also be tasked to conduct EMIO. EMIO are authorized by the President through SecDef to deter, degrade, disrupt, or prevent attacks against the US and its allies. EMIO involve interception of targeted personnel or materiel that poses an imminent threat to the US and its allies. EMIO may be implemented without sanctions and may involve multinational forces. USN ships must be augmented by other forces (e.g., Navy SEALs or specially trained Marines) to conduct high freeboard noncompliant boardings or to conduct opposed boardings.

*For further reference see, NTTP 3-07.11/Coast Guard Publication (CGP) 3-07.11,* Maritime Interception Operations. *See also JP 3-03,* Joint Interdiction.

(8) **Littoral Operations.** Maritime security in the littoral regions is attained through use of a defensive sea area in which forces are employed to protect use of designated offshore coastal areas by friendly forces and to deny the use of those areas to enemy forces.

c. **Air Operations in Homeland Defense Operations.** NORAD is assigned the mission of aerospace control (includes air sovereignty and air defense) of the airspace of the US and Canada. NORAD routinely maintains forces on alert for homeland air defense, cruise missile defense, and aerospace control alert missions against long-range incursions. Air and missile defenses are discussed under Paragraph 6, "Protection." USNORTHCOM is generally responsible for all other air operations supporting land and maritime HD outside the scope of the NORAD Agreement.

(1) NORAD/US element to NORAD should also be prepared to intercept and defend against terrorist air threats, even when the intent to harm the US is uncertain. These threats could include commercial or chartered aircraft, general aviation, ultra light aerial vehicles, unmanned aerial systems (include commercial to radio-controlled aircraft) or even balloons. Early detection and successful interception of these types of potential threats requires cooperation and very close coordination with interagency partners, including FAA and DHS.

(2) Aerospace defense operations within the homeland provide some unique concerns for commanders with geographic HD responsibilities, CDRUSNORTHCOM and CDRUSPACOM.

(a) **Size.** The GCCs' HD responsibilities include vast areas of airspace, land masses, and water. In particular, North America is a huge land mass with multiple avenues of approach that an adversary could use to advantage.

(b) **Control of Airspace.** US airspace is under the control of the FAA. Civilian control of airspace, as well as other security functions vital to the homeland, requires coordination among several major government agencies.

(c) **Peacetime Environment.** Operations must be conducted in peacetime, as well as in times of crisis.

(d) **Duration.** Defense of the homeland is continuous, involving US and Canadian air, land, and maritime forces, on a 24/7 operational basis in peacetime as well as in times of crisis. It will continue for the foreseeable future.

(e) **Rules of Engagement.** The airspace environment over areas of the homeland is dense. For example, there may be up to 5,000 aircraft at a given time over CONUS. ONE operates with strict ROE in this very dense airspace. The ROE for operating in US airspace often produce a constrained engagement environment.

(3) SecDef has designated CDRNORAD as the supported commander for aerospace warning and aerospace control aspects of HD within the NORAD OA.

(a) Aerospace warning consists of surveillance, detection, validation, and warning of an attack against North America, whether by aircraft, missiles or space vehicles. Aerospace control consists of air sovereignty and air defense operations within US and Canadian airspace.

(b) The OA includes the portions of the homeland that fall within the USNORTHCOM AOR, specifically CONUS, Alaska, the US Virgin Islands, and Puerto Rico. CDRUSPACOM is the designated CCDR for HD missions within the USPACOM AOR. CDRUSNORTHCOM is the supported CCDR for HD missions within the USNORTHCOM AOR that are not under the direction of CDRNORAD.

(4) The missions of NORAD and USNORTHCOM are complementary. NORAD conducts missions and operations within the USNORTHCOM AOR and provides warning of all airborne threats, to include aircraft and missile attack, as well as threats existing in the maritime domain. USNORTHCOM conducts US-only air, land, and maritime defense. The commands work side-by-side and coordinate on many issues. NORAD is an integral part of an active layered defense that relies on the early warning of an emerging threat to quickly deploy and execute a decisive response. NORAD plays a critical role in the air and space defense of Canada and HD of the US by providing aerospace warning and airspace control and maritime warning for North America.

(a) **Operation NOBLE EAGLE.** ONE is the operation covering aerospace warning and control aspects of HD for CONUS, Alaska, the US Virgin Islands, and Puerto Rico. As the binational element of this operation, NORAD is tasked to support ONE by employing the forces and C2 necessary to protect these areas from air attack. USPACOM provides C2 (through Pacific Air Forces) for ONE support to Hawaii and Guam.

(b) The authority and decision to engage is made at the highest levels of command. NORAD constantly refines its procedures as necessary and coordinates with DHS, Public Safety Canada, Emergency Preparedness Canada, the FAA and its Canadian equivalent NAV CANADA [air traffic control agency], and with civilian LE organizations and other government agencies within the US and Canada.

*For a more complete description of the NORAD missions, organization, and structure see Appendix C, "North American Aerospace Defense Command, Missions, Organization, and Structure." For more information, refer to NORAD CONPLAN 3310.*

d. **Space Operations in the Conduct of Homeland Defense.** The region in space above the US and other countries cannot be owned or possessed like territory. However, it is USG policy that purposeful interference with US space systems will be viewed as an infringement on the Nation's sovereign rights. In order to deter or preempt attacks and to protect military space assets, DOD conducts space operations in support of HD. DOD DCI activities may be closely related to military space operations, given that selected space capabilities may be classified as DCI. These activities may serve to protect and defend the US's ability to operate in and through space. CDRUSSTRATCOM is the supported commander for protecting and defending the right to operate in space and is responsible for identifying, assessing, and securing DOD critical assets in space.

(1) **Enabling Capabilities.** Military space operations bring enabling capabilities and information to the JFC. For example, initial threat detections and locations, global communication, real-time weather, high-resolution imagery and signals intelligence (SIGINT) help the JFC determine the appropriate intercept vehicle, location, and/or time of attack. Using the global communication capability, the JFC is able to exercise real-time C2 functions and post-mission assessment. Satellite communications (SATCOM) technology can link HD forces with interagency, intergovernmental, and other federal and state, tribal, and local partners in support of HD operations. This information from space systems provides decision makers advance warning to prevent, prepare for, respond to, and recover from threats to the homeland.

(2) **Roles and Responsibilities**

(a) CDRUSSTRATCOM is responsible for developing desired characteristics and capabilities, advocating, planning, and conducting space operations (force enhancement, space control, and space support, including space lift and on-orbit operations and force application). These responsibilities are to:

1. Provide warning and assessment of space attack.

2. Support NORAD by providing the missile warning and space surveillance necessary to fulfill the US commitment to the NORAD Agreement.

3. Serve as the single point of contact for military space operational matters, except as otherwise directed.

4. Provide military representation to US national agencies, commercial entities, and international agencies for matters related to military space operations. This will be as directed and in coordination with CJCS and other CCDRs.

5. Coordinate and conduct space campaign planning.

(b) CDRUSSTRATCOM established the JFCC SPACE to serve as the single point of contact for operational space matters, including planning, tasking, directing, and executing space operations using assigned space forces.

(c) GCCs with geographic HD responsibilities have specific responsibilities for HD and are the supported commanders responsible for conducting HD operations within their respective AORs. These include:

1. Communicate space capability requirements through the command's SCA to JFCC SPACE when acting in an HD capacity.

2. Provide FP for space assets located within their respective AORs.

(3) **Integration of Civilian Space Capabilities.** HD is a high-priority activity which requires the marshalling of all available space capabilities. Key to maximizing US space capabilities is the successful integration of civilian space assets with military space

capabilities. In many cases, especially in the area of SATCOM, environmental monitoring, and some space imagery, the contribution of civilian systems provides an integral part of the total US space capabilities. The private sector and other civilian space capabilities are essential to the effectiveness of the US's ability to successfully accomplish the HD mission.

*For additional information, refer to JP 3-14,* Space Operations.

e. **Cyberspace Operations in the Conduct of Homeland Defense.** The US conducts operations, including HD, in a complex, interconnected, and increasingly global operational environment. Cyberspace is a global domain within the information environment consisting of the interdependent network of information technology infrastructures and resident data, including the Internet, telecommunications networks, computer systems, and embedded processors and controllers.

(1) **The NMS for Cyberspace Operations** offers a comprehensive military strategy for DOD to enhance US military strategic superiority in cyberspace. The NMS for Cyberspace Operations addresses three main roles: defense of the nation; national incident response; and critical infrastructure protection. GCCs with geographic HD responsibilities should ensure unified action at the theater level for cyberspace operations. This includes coordinating with coalition and interagency partners as outlined in strategy, policy, and agreements. JFCs employ cyberspace capabilities to achieve objectives in or through cyberspace. Such operations include offensive cyberspace operations, defensive cyberspace operations, and DOD information network operations.

(2) The security and effective operations of US critical infrastructure—including energy, banking and finance, transportation, communication, and the DIB—rely on cyberspace (e.g., industrial control systems, and information technology are vulnerable to disruption or exploitation).

*For additional information, refer to JP 3-12,* Cyberspace Operations.

f. **The Information Environment in the Conduct of Homeland Defense**

(1) The information environment supports the HD framework. This environment is the aggregate of individuals, organizations, or systems that collect, process, disseminate, or act on information. Also included in this environment is the information itself. The information environment is broad in scope and directly supports military operations in any operational environment. It offers a framework of three dimensions: physical, informational, and cognitive. The integrated employment, during military operations, of information-related capabilities in concert with other lines of operation to influence, disrupt, corrupt, or usurp the decision making of adversaries and potential adversaries while protecting our own is known as information operations (IO).

*Details on the planning of IO can be found in JP 3-13,* Information Operations.

(2) **DOD Information Networks (DODIN).** As part of the overall information environment, DODIN represent the globally interconnected communications system of DOD. They include the end-to-end set of information capabilities, associated processes, and

personnel for collecting, processing, storing, disseminating and managing information on demand to warfighters, policy makers, and support personnel. The DOD information networks include all owned and leased communications and computing systems and services, software (including applications), data, security services, and other associated services.

(a) Consistent with laws and policy, Services, DOD agencies, and non-DOD agencies should provide capabilities to support CCMD requirements to ensure the interoperability, availability, and shared situational awareness and understanding of the HD information environment. This includes capabilities to detect, deter, prevent, and defeat virtual and physical attacks against defense information network infrastructure that directly or indirectly supports HD missions.

(b) There are three primary aspects to providing available and effective systems with which to operate in an HD information environment. These are: providing a reliable, robust HD communication system; improving information sharing among HD mission partners; and assuring and defending the critical defense information network infrastructure against threats and aggression.

*For more information on cyberspace operations, see JP 3-12,* Cyberspace Operations, *and JP 6-0,* Joint Communications System.

1. The communications system enables centralized planning and the coordinated and mutually supporting employment of forces and assets. It includes command centers, operations centers, processing and distribution centers and their associated systems, deployed systems, and data sources. Systems or information, and decisions generated by them, should be shared to the maximum extent possible to ensure synchronization of effort among mission partners. For example, the common operational picture (COP) facilitates decentralized execution in rapidly changing operational environments and should be shared among appropriate agencies, to include LE, to ensure consistent situational awareness.

2. Commercial infrastructure plays a critical role in enabling the communication systems that directly support HD operations. This infrastructure may be damaged to the point that military and supporting operations are adversely affected. DOD must identify capabilities that can help bridge the gap until local infrastructure is restored. These capabilities must be highly mobile, rapidly deployable, and commercially interoperable.

3. The GCC AORs are rich with existing commercial communications systems that can be leveraged to the maximum extent possible. For example, commercial cellular capabilities represent a choice medium that can provide immediate capability. DOD communications systems will serve as the backbone in support of HD operations. Systems that are scalable, interoperable, and complementary with those used by multinational and civilian partners, will be essential to augment traditional ISR and C2 nodes, especially in the early phases of military operations. These communications must be mobile, secure, and voice and data capable. Wireless voice, data, and video are critical to effective C2. Planning for the integration of spectrum resource allocation will enable DOD, federal, state, local and tribal responders, IGOs and NGOs, and private sector responders to operate on the same

bandwidth, to facilitate interoperability. Planning for the integration of internationally-donated telecommunications resources, including hardware and SATCOM bandwidth, must be conducted in the event the USG accepts offers of international aid.

*For more information on spectrum management, see JP 6-01,* Joint Electromagnetic Spectrum Management Operations.

## 6. Protection

The protection function focuses on conserving the joint force's fighting potential in four primary ways: **active defensive** measures that protect the joint force, its information, its bases, necessary infrastructure, and lines of communications from an adversary's attack; **passive defensive** measures that make friendly forces, systems, and facilities difficult to locate, strike, and destroy; **application of technology and procedures** to reduce the risk of friendly fire; and **emergency management and response** to reduce the loss of personnel and capabilities due to accidents. It includes, but extends beyond, FP to encompass protection of US noncombatants; the forces, systems, and civil infrastructure of friendly nations; and other government departments and agencies, IGOs, and NGOs. Planning for HD includes combating terrorism, criminal enterprises, environmental threats/hazards, and cyberspace attacks. **Joint intelligence preparation of the operational environment must be conducted to ensure adequate planning and implementation of protection measures.**

*For additional information on the protection function see JP 3-0,* Joint Operations. *For more information on DOD AT and FP programs, refer to DODI 2000.12,* DOD Antiterrorism Program, *DODI 2000.16,* DOD Antiterrorism Standards, *and JP 3-07.2,* Antiterrorism.

a. **Integrated Air and Missile Defense (IAMD).** IAMD is the integration of capabilities and overlapping operations to defend the homeland and United States national interests, protect the joint force, and enable freedom of action by negating the adversary's ability to create adverse effects from their air and missile capabilities. Key to detecting and countering air and missile threats is sensor integration. CDRUSNORTHCOM is also normally designated CDRNORAD. USNORTHCOM, USPACOM, and NORAD share the missions of air defense and missile defense for the homeland. NORAD is tasked to provide aerospace warning for North America, to include the detection, validation, and warning of an attack, whether by aircraft, missiles, or space vehicles. CDRNORAD is also tasked to provide the aerospace control for North America, which includes surveillance and control of Canadian and US airspace, as well as ensuring air sovereignty and air defense against aircraft and cruise missiles (CMs). CDRUSNORTHCOM is the supported commander for BMD and all other HD within the AOR not under direction of CDRNORAD. CDRUSPACOM is responsible for HD within the USPACOM AOR, including air and missile defense. USPACOM supports USNORTHCOM for certain limited defense options for BMD. CDRUSSTRATCOM is responsible for synchronizing global missile defense planning, in addition to coordinating global missile defense operations support.

*For further discussions on missile defense, refer to JP 3-01,* Countering Air and Missile Threats.

(1) **Cruise Missile Defense.** Without an extreme triggering event, it is unlikely that any nation with CMs would strike the US homeland, because of the implications of the US strategic deterrence defense posture.

(a) **Sea-Launched Cruise Missiles (SLCMs).** SLCMs are capable of delivering a full range of warheads, from conventional to WMD. From an HD standpoint, SLCMs are a concern because they may be launched from the sea with little advance notice. However, the most likely threat is from a terrorist group with a covert SLCM capability that can be launched from a merchant vessel.

(b) **Air-Launched Cruise Missiles (ALCMs).** ALCMs present significant detection difficulties due to standoff range and very small radar cross-section. From an HD perspective, the practical defense is targeting the airfields from which the ALCM-capable aircraft are launched. It is highly unlikely a terrorist organization could utilize an ALCM capability.

(c) A terrorist attack using an aircraft as the weapon, as done in September 2001 continues to be the most likely air threat to the homeland.

(2) **Ballistic Missile Defense.** BMD capabilities are designed to detect, deter, prevent, and defeat adversary ballistic missile threats, and help protect the US domestic population and critical infrastructure. US homeland BMD strategy includes not only the means for active and passive defenses, but the capability to strike in retaliation or to preempt the launch of a missile threat. For HD there are BMD capabilities against a very limited attack by a rogue state using an ICBM, and capabilities against threats from short-range ballistic missiles (SRBMs), medium-range ballistic missiles (MRBMs), and intermediate-range ballistic missiles (IRBMs). ICBM threats from major adversarial powers are deterred by US counterforce capabilities that include global strike. BMD is a key element of HD, however, BMD activities do not include defense against cruise or tactical air-to-surface missiles.

(a) **Ballistic Missile Defense System (BMDS).** BMDS includes the sensors (air, land, sea, and space), communications, and C2 for launch warnings and assessment for all categories of ballistic missile launches, whether targeted against the homeland or other AORs.

(b) **Command Roles and Responsibilities.** All CCMDs are tasked with deterring attacks against the US and its territories, and employing appropriate force should deterrence fail within their respective AORs. GCCs are responsible for planning and executing BMD against ballistic missile threats that target their AORs, to include threats that cross AOR boundaries. This is supported by shared situational awareness, integrated battle management C2, adaptive planning, and accurate and responsive battle damage assessment. The following have specific BMD responsibilities to support HD.

1. USNORTHCOM and USPACOM have specified HD responsibilities and authority to deter ballistic missile attacks on the US, its territories and bases within the respective AORs, and other areas as directed by the President or SecDef. In coordination

with CDRUSSTRATCOM and other GCCs, they synchronize support for the execution of operational plans to detect, deter, prevent, and defeat ballistic missile attacks on the homeland, and should deterrence fail and/or as directed by the President or SecDef, they employ BMD forces in a synchronized operation to protect the US against ballistic missile attacks. CDRUSNORTHCOM, in coordination with CDRUSPACOM, has certain responsibilities within the USPACOM AOR to ensure a seamless homeland BMD. Homeland BMD using the ground-based midcourse defense (GMD) requires centralized planning and direction by CDRUSNORTHCOM and centralized execution with positive direction from the weapons release authority (WRA). WRA is the authority delegated from the President to use certain weapons (e.g., ground-based interceptors) against ICBM threats. USPACOM supports USNORTHCOM and the WRA for homeland BMD using GMD, and within the USPACOM AOR, CDRUSPACOM is the supported commander for homeland BMD that does not include GMD.

      2. CDRUSSTRATCOM serves as a global synchronizer for global missile defense planning and is responsible to:

      a. Synchronize, plan, and coordinate support for global missile defense operations.

      b. Provide missile warning and space surveillance to NORAD to fulfill the US commitment to the NORAD Agreement.

      c. Provide warning of missile attack to all other CCDRs, and provide assessment of missile attack if the appropriate CCMD is unable to do so.

      d. Develop the concept of operations for global missile defense.

      e. Support other CCMDs in the development, assessment, coordination, and recommendation of BMD.

      3. CDRUSSTRATCOM established the Joint Functional Component Command for Integrated Missile Defense (JFCC-IMD) to optimize planning, execution, force management, and coordination with other CCMDs for USSTRATCOM's global missile defense mission. JFCC-IMD coordinates activities with associated GCC, other USSTRATCOM joint functional component commands, the Services, and the efforts of the Missile Defense Agency (MDA) to accomplish CDRUSSTRATCOM UCP assigned tasks.

(3) **Space Operations and BMD.** Space operations are considered critical enabling activities for BMD. For example, space based surveillance and sensor capabilities provide ballistic missile early warning, assist in intelligence gathering, and facilitate tracking inbound missiles.

*For further space operation considerations reference JP 3-14,* Space Operations.

(4) **National Capital Region-Integrated Air Defense System.** DOD employs an integrated air defense system (sensors, weapons, visual warning system, C2 systems, and personnel) as part of the around-the-clock, multilayered, joint military and interagency effort.

(a) The NCR-IADS augments the ONE fighter defenses by providing assets in-place which are in a quick reaction posture to protect the seat of the USG, as well as other key locations in the NCR from air attacks.

(b) TSA and other elements of DHS, as well as DOJ and DOT, conduct significant aviation security efforts throughout the US and in the NCR. Principal among the efforts designed to improve interagency coordination is the National Capital Region Coordination Center (NCRCC), sponsored by TSA. The NCRCC enhances interagency coordination by providing a venue for representatives of the many organizations with a stake in the defense of the NCR to "stand watch" together. Through the NCRCC, various agencies have improved situational awareness regarding the actions of their defense partners. The NCRCC is a "coordination center"—no command or control of forces occurs. NCRCC participants include the FBI, TSA, FAA, US Capitol Police, US Secret Service, US Customs and Border Protection Office of Air and Marine Operations, USCG, JFHQ-NCR, and NORAD. Representatives from other state and local LEAs and the Joint Air Defense Operations Center (JADOC) also participate at the NCRCC when threats or circumstances warrant.

*For additional information on the full range of air operations, consult the following doctrinal publications: JP 3-01,* Countering Air and Missile Threats; *JP 3-09.3,* Close Air Support; *JP 3-17,* Air Mobility Operations; *JP 3-30,* Command and Control for Joint Air Operations, *and JP 3-52,* Joint Airspace Control.

b. **Critical Infrastructure Protection**

(1) **Defense Critical Infrastructure.** DCI consists of the DOD and non-DOD networked assets essential to project, support, and sustain military forces and operations worldwide. Assets are people, physical entities, or information. Physical assets include infrastructure such as installations, facilities, ports, bridges, power stations, telecommunication lines and pipelines, most of which will not be located on USG property.

(a) The DCIP complements other DOD programs and efforts, such as FP, AT, information assurance, and COOP. In carrying out the functions of the Homeland Security Act of 2002, the roles and responsibilities of the Secretary of HS are further defined in HSPD-7, Critical Infrastructure Identification, Prioritization, and Protection, to include the coordination and overall national effort to enhance the protection of the CI/KR of the US. One exception is the DIB, which falls under DOD as the sector specific agency for coordinating its protection.

(b) Examples of DCI include strategic military bases, ports of embarkation/ports of debarkation, mobilization staging and storage areas, plus rail and trucking transportation centers. Protection and defense of non-DOD facilities is normally coordinated with federal, state, tribal, and local LEAs; however, if directed by the President, DOD may be tasked to provide the forces and have the overall responsibility to defend these facilities. HD includes the protection of critical DOD networks and when directed, national networks against threats and aggression. This includes DOD critical information infrastructure. It is accomplished through physical and virtual protection. State and local governments also are interested in securing critical infrastructure/key resources (CI/KR), so coordination of physical/virtual protection measures should be part of the USG efforts.

(c) **National Guard Critical Infrastructure Protection (NG CIP) Teams.** NG-CIP and NG cyberspace CIP teams assess industrial sites and critical USG infrastructure for vulnerabilities to attack. These teams support the DOD and DHS by conducting all-hazard vulnerability assessments of prioritized DIB and DHS-Tier II sites.

(d) **Mission Assurance and the DIB.** Mission assurance focuses on the "protection," "continued function," and "rapid reconstitution" of critical assets which support mission essential functions, rather than the execution of these missions themselves. Mission assurance is a common integrative framework, not a policy or program, to prioritize protection and resiliency efforts and reduce the US's vulnerability to a range of complex threats and hazards. Mission assurance should leverage existing protection and resilience programs, such as AT, physical security, COOP, CIP, and information assurance, and provide input to existing DOD planning, budget, requirements, and acquisition processes. Threats to non-DOD government and commercially owned infrastructure, facilities, and capabilities, to include the DIB, can jeopardize DOD HD mission execution. A mission assurance strategy focused only on assessing and protecting, or enhancing resilience against DOD-specific vulnerabilities will fail. Thus, it is necessary to comprehensively assess and mitigate risk in a way that accounts for DOD dependence on civilian assets and systems and the cascading consequences of their disruption. These include, but are not limited to, transportation networks, global supply chains, electric power, telecommunications, and information technology infrastructures. Simultaneously, one must also recognize the lead role of other USG departments and agencies, especially DHS, the Department of Energy (DOE), and DOT, in coordinating risk mitigation strategies for threats to civilian infrastructure.

(e) **CCDRs conducting HD missions are responsible for establishing a DCIP that conforms to DOD requirements and policy.** DOD components are also responsible for establishing similar programs. This is done by identifying and assessing the critical assets and infrastructure dependencies that are necessary for the successful execution of present and projected military operations, their fulfillment of HD operations, and protection of US interests at home. Components also address these issues at the installation level. Installation level mission assurance assessments must consider the impact that degradation or loss of the supporting off-installation critical infrastructure would have on DOD operations. Examples are water, power, communications, and transportation facilities.

*For more information concerning CIP and the DCIP, see DODD 3020.40,* DOD Policy and Responsibility for Critical Infrastructure, *and DODI 5220.22,* National Industrial Security Program.

(2) **Critical Infrastructure and Key Resources.** As stated in the Critical Infrastructure and Key Resources Support Annex to the National Response Framework (NRF), "CI/KR includes those assets, systems, networks, and functions-physical or virtual–so vital to the US that their incapacitation or destruction would have a debilitating impact on security, national economic security, public health or safety, or any combination of those matters. Key resources are publicly or privately controlled resources essential to minimal

operation of the economy and the government." An attack on CI/KR could significantly disrupt the functioning of government and business alike, and produce cascading effects far beyond the physical location of the incident. The federal government facilitates expedited information sharing and analysis of impacts to CI/KR, prioritized recommendations, and processes to consider incident-related requests for assistance from CI/KR owners and operators. The NRF implements the national policy for comprehensive, national, all-hazards approach to domestic incident response. It identifies special circumstances where the USG exercises a larger role, including incidents where federal interests are involved and catastrophic incidents where a state would require significant support. The National Infrastructure Protection Plan implements the national policy for CI/KR protection.

*For further information, see HSPD-5,* Management of Domestic Incidents, *HSPD-7,* Critical Infrastructure Identification, Prioritization, and Protection; the National Strategy for Physical Protection of Critical Infrastructure and Key Assets; the National Infrastructure Protection Plan; *and HSPD-23,* Cyber Security and Monitoring. *See also the NRF (http://www.fema.gov/pdf/emergency/nrf/nrf-core.pdf).*

   c. **Countering Weapons of Mass Destruction**

   (1) Adversary WMD capabilities are of particular concern to the USG. Adversaries may use WMD as a tool to inflict mass casualties on homeland civilian populations or cause disruption or destruction to critical infrastructure.

   (2) CWMD as a part of HD is a global mission with immense potential consequences which cross AOR boundaries, requires an integrated and synchronized effort, and requires numerous interagency and multinational partners for effective mission accomplishment. Rather than a discrete, specialized mission, CWMD requires a continuous campaign conducted and supported by the entire USG. CCDRs with HD equities will often be acting in support of another LFA, or even supporting a multinational effort.

   (3) CWMD contributes to HD through an integrated approach to detect, deter, prevent, and defeat those who seek to harm the US, its allies, partners, and interests by using CBRN weapons.

*For more information on CWMD see JP 3-40,* Countering Weapons of Mass Destruction, *JP 3-41,* Chemical, Biological, Radiological, and Nuclear Consequence Management, *and JP 3-11,* Operations in Chemical, Biological, Radiological, and Nuclear (CBRN) Environments.

   d. **Cyberspace Operations—DOD Information Networks Operations.** Protection of US national infrastructure and its cyberspace systems is provided through a layered defense. DHS has overall responsibility for cybersecurity of US national infrastructure. Each CCMD, Service, and DOD agency contributes to overall HD cybersecurity by rigorous implementation of cybersecurity policies and procedures. CCMDs, Services, and agencies employ appropriate cyberspace defenses to prevent intrusions and defeat adversary activities on DOD networks and systems. Protection of the DODIN is led by USCYBERCOM and supported by DISA and the National Security Agency (NSA). The IC Incident Response Center is the single focal point for IC network incident reporting and management.

Activities involving IC networks, specifically sensitive compartmented information networks, will be coordinated IAW joint procedures approved by SecDef and the Director of National Intelligence. Due to the close interdependencies that DOD and IC components have on each other's networks, it is essential that reporting procedures be in place to ensure rapid coordination in network defense. Reporting on IC networks is accomplished through USCYBERCOM and shared with the CCDRs with geographic HD responsibilities.

*For more information on cyberspace operations, see JP 3-12, Cyberspace Operations.*

   e. **Force Protection.** GCCs are responsible for FP within their AORs. FP includes actions taken to prevent or mitigate hostile actions against DOD personnel (to include family members), resources, facilities, and critical information. It does not include actions to defeat the enemy or protect against accidents, weather, or disease. All GCCs have FP responsibilities, including those with AORs which contain geographic areas of the homeland. Force health protection (FHP), the protection component of health services, complements FP and includes all measures to provide for the health and safety of Service members.

   (1) **Antiterrorism and Force Protection.** GCCs have overall AT responsibility within their AOR, except for those DOD elements and personnel for whom another commander has security responsibility pursuant to law or an MOA. The AT program is designed to prevent and detect terrorist attacks against DOD personnel, their families, facilities, resources, installations, and DCI, as well as to prepare to defend against, and plan the response to the consequences of terrorist incidents. TACON (for FP) applies to all DOD personnel assigned, permanently or temporarily, transiting through, or performing exercises or training in the GCC's AOR. GCCs have the authority to modify FP conditions for covered individuals. CDRUSNORTHCOM has overall DOD AT program and FP responsibility in CONUS. USNORTHCOM's FP mission and AT program are outlined in the USNORTHCOM Instruction 10-222, Force Protection Mission and Antiterrorism Program.

*For additional information see JP 3-07.2, Antiterrorism.*

   (2) **Force Health Protection.** FHP provides the framework for optimizing health readiness and protecting Service members from all health threats. In general, US states and territories in the AORs of the GCCs with geographic HD responsibilities are normally at low risk for endemic diseases, although, pandemic disease outbreaks have the potential to rapidly place the US military and wider population at risk. Additionally, some physical areas of the homeland are heavily industrialized and have the potential for the deliberate or accidental release of a large variety of toxic industrial chemicals/materials at production sites and during transportation. Furthermore, WMD or CBRN attacks pose unique FHP measures due to the medical effects and threats of CBRN agents. Thus, man-made hazards (deliberate or accidental) may present the greatest potential health risk to forces conducting HD operations.

*For more on FHP, see JP 4-02, Health Services.*

f. **Combating terrorism** includes AT and CT actions taken to oppose terrorism throughout the entire threat spectrum. The USG policy on combating terrorism is to defeat violent extremism and create a global environment that is inhospitable to violent extremists. The broad USG strategy is to continue to lead an international effort to deny violent extremist networks the resources and functions they need to operate and survive. CT actions are those taken directly and indirectly against terrorist networks to influence and render global and regional environments inhospitable to terrorist organizations in order to prevent, deter, disrupt, or destroy terrorist operations before they strike at the homeland. SOF maintain core competencies in counterinsurgency (COIN) and CT operations. The DOD strategy for combating terrorism implements the following objectives from the National Strategy for Combating Terrorism, which are derived from the National Security Strategy (NSS):

(1) Thwart or defeat terrorist attacks against the US, its partner nations (PNs), and its interests.

(2) Attack and disrupt terrorist networks abroad so as to cause adversaries to be incapable or unwilling to attack the US homeland, allies, or interests.

(3) Deny terrorist networks WMD

(4) Establish conditions that allow PNs to govern their territory effectively and defeat terrorists.

(5) Deny a hospitable environment to violent extremists.

*COIN and CT are discussed in detail in JP 3-24,* Counterinsurgency Operations, *and JP 3-26,* Counterterrorism.

7. **Sustainment**

a. **Personnel**

(1) The core functional responsibilities of the manpower and personnel directorate of a joint staff (J-1) are accomplished during any HD or other operation and are tailored to meet mission specific requirements.

(2) **Personnel Support.** The authorities and responsibilities for personnel support to HD operations are largely the same as those for any other DOD mission set. Some exceptions may apply to the USNORTHCOM AOR.

(a) **Personnel Accountability.** Personnel accountability is a command responsibility. Personnel accountability, strength reporting, and manpower management are the focal points for a joint force J-1 during HD operations. HD operations in CONUS pose specific challenges. For example, units deploy from their home stations instead of from a unique designated port of debarkation. Service personnel elements supporting home station deployments must ensure that all processing and reporting requirements are met prior to unit deployment. In specific circumstances, such as operations in a WMD environment, the employing CJTF may establish a joint personnel reception center to ensure arriving units are ready for employment, but this would be the exception.

(b) **Individual Augmentation.** The GCC's forces are task organized when needed, causing a potential requirement for augmentation. Tactical capabilities are provided by organic unit force structure wherever possible, and the request vehicle for this type of requirement is the RFF. Individual subject matter experts may be required to augment operational C2 organizations. The request vehicle for joint individual augmentation is a CCDR-approved and Joint Staff-validated joint manning document. Joint individual augmentees are not QRFs, but are a result of deliberate planning for contingencies, if the contingency for the unique task organization is projected to last longer than 90-120 days. See CJCSI 1301.01, *Joint Individual Augmentation Procedures,* for detailed guidance.

(c) **Personnel Accountability in Conjunction with Disasters.** Attacks on the US can affect DOD personnel and their dependents. Service components account for and report the status of all DOD-affiliated military and civilian personnel, including contractor and all family members immediately following a disaster or attack. Additionally, Service components should be prepared to report the number of Service members, DOD civilians, DOD contractors, and their dependents requiring evacuation from an affected area.

*See DODI 3001.02,* Personnel Accountability in Conjunction With Natural or Man-made Disasters. *For detailed guidance on personnel support, see JP 1-0,* Joint Personnel Support.

b. **Logistics.** The authorities and responsibilities for logistics operations in support of HD are largely the same as any other DOD mission set. Some notable exceptions, however, apply to HD operations within the US. More specifically, the exceptions apply to the USNORTHCOM AOR.

(1) JP 1, *Doctrine for the Armed Forces of the United States,* states that the "exercise of directive authority for logistics (DAFL) by a CCDR includes the authority to delegate authority for a common support capability to subordinate commanders" and that "CCDRs exercise COCOM over assigned forces." Within the USNORTHCOM AOR the CDRUSNORTHCOM does not have assigned forces and therefore executes OPCON or TACON over attached forces without DAFL. Given the robust logistics capabilities within each Service component and DOD support agency/commercial contracting infrastructure in the USNORTHCOM AOR, DAFL is generally not necessary for CDRUSNORTHCOM to execute the HD mission. However, it may be necessary at times for CDRUSNORTHCOM to exercise DAFL in responding to an HD threat, or more specifically, in reacting in the aftermath of an actual attack against the homeland. For such instances, the President or SecDef may extend this authority to attached forces when transferring those forces for a specific mission.

(2) Implementation and execution of logistics functions remain the responsibility of the Services and the Service component commanders. Each Service is responsible for the logistics support of its own forces, except when logistics support is otherwise provided for by agreements with national agencies, allies, or another Service.

(3) In the case where multiple logistics capabilities from many participating agencies, partner nations, IGOs, NGOs, and private sector entities are involved in HD operations, each is ultimately responsible for providing logistics support for their own personnel. However, the GCC should strive to integrate efforts through the use of acquisition and cross-servicing agreements and associated implementing arrangements and any other vehicle necessary to ensure needed logistics support. Optimizing the capabilities should result in greater flexibility, more options, and more effective logistics support. In allocation of logistics support to HD activities, the unit force activity designators should be reviewed for possible improvement or downgrade based on mission criticality.

(4) **Logistic Capabilities.** Responsibilities for logistics as described in JP 4-0, *Joint Logistics,* apply to HD operations as follows:

(a) **Supply.** USNORTHCOM will normally not establish supply buildup rates or determine theater stockage levels in the USNORTHCOM AOR. Based on mission requirements, Service components and DOD combat support agencies (CSAs) determine build up rates and stockage levels for supply.

(b) **Maintenance Operations.** Service components and CSAs will maintain administrative and coordination responsibilities for maintenance operations within the USNORTHCOM AOR.

(c) **Deployment and Distribution.** HD airlift priorities are outlined in CJCSI 4120.02, *Assignment of Movement and Mobilization Priority.* The national importance of included mission areas is reflected in the elevated movement priorities that can be applied for these missions by the President or SecDef. For operations that demand expedited movement, CDRUSTRANSCOM maintains on-call readiness levels necessary to meet CDRUSNORTHCOM mission requirements. The NORAD and USNORTHCOM Deployment and Distribution Operations Cell (NDDOC) is embedded within the Joint Logistics Operations Center and is composed of personnel from NORAD and USNORTHCOM and national partners as required (i.e., US Transportation Command (USTRANSCOM), Defense Logistics Agency (DLA), the Services, and other organizations). It is established as directed by CDRUSNORTHCOM to support HD (and DSCA) operations and operates under the direction of the NORAD and USNORTHCOM logistics and engineering directorate. The NDDOC implements command movement priorities, anticipates and resolves transportation shortfalls, prioritizes transportation assets, synchronizes deployment force flow and distribution, and provides in-transit visibility.

(d) **Combat Service Support (CSS).** CSS is a Service responsibility. It enhances combat capability and improves productivity by providing life-sustaining and essential services and critical supply, maintenance, and transportation services to enable the operating force to conduct HD missions, supporting force reception and beddown during military operations. The primary focus of the CSS effort in HD is to sustain and assist employed DOD forces.

(5) **Joint Reception, Staging, Onward Movement, and Integration (JRSOI).** JRSOI is defined by the operational commander and is the essential process that assembles

## BASE SUPPORT INSTALLATION (BSI)

**A BSI, when approved by the Secretary of Defense, serves as the main logistical hub for military support operations. Although joint forces may arrive through multiple reception sites near the joint operating area, generally the logistics support is provided by the BSI. Typically, most forces will deploy through, and the majority of sustainment will be positioned at the BSI. A BSI will normally have the following characteristics: a logistics requisitioning activity, an airfield (or nearby airport) and communications infrastructure sufficient to meet the surge of forces into an operational area, dry open areas for staging of supplies and equipment, a good road network, health and other life support services to include billeting, food service and force protection and be close to the joint operating area to remain responsive and flexible to the needs of the joint force.**

deploying forces keep consisting of personnel, equipment, and materiel arriving in theater, into forces capable of meeting the CCDR's operational requirements. For HD operations within the USNORTHCOM AOR, the personnel, equipment, and materiel will likely originate from within the JOA. In the USNORTHCOM AOR, portions of JRSOI identified below, are not regarded as discrete steps necessary for HD operations.

(a) JRSOI for a large force can/will most likely require resources beyond that of the designated base support installation (BSI). The supported CCDR should request sufficient JRSOI support to ensure that the designated BSI can perform JRSOI.

(b) Reception operations include all those functions required to receive and clear unit personnel, equipment, and materiel through the BSI or reception area. For HD operations within the USNORTHCOM AOR, the personnel, equipment, and materiel will likely originate from within the JOA. In that case, personnel, equipment, and materiel are already accounted for at the home base, making the home base essentially the point of departure. Component support plans will address processes for in place personnel reporting to the CJTF.

(c) Similar to reception, personnel, equipment, and materiel to be employed for HD operations within the USNORTHCOM AOR may stage within the confines of their home installation. Otherwise, arriving personnel, equipment, and personnel may be temporarily held at a BSI or other location while they are staged, assembled, and organized in preparation for onward movement.

(d) Onward movement is the process of moving units and accompanying materiel from reception facilities, marshalling areas, and staging areas to tactical assembly areas (TAAs) and/or OAs or other theater destinations. Because units and forces employed in HD operations within the USNORTHCOM AOR are likely to be geographically close to the JOAs, the TAA can be located at the unit's or force's home base. Onward movement, in many instances, can be accomplished concurrently/collocated with reception and staging activities at the home base. When a unit or force is not geographically close to an OA and a

TAA other than the home base is desired, then discrete, onward movement activities would be required. Oftentimes, a TAA would be located at a designated BSI that would provide logistics support and be located near the OA.

(e) Integration is the synchronized hand off of units into an operational commander's force prior to mission execution. HD operations within the USNORTHCOM AOR often require complex C2 structures, thus special attention to integration is required. Refer to Appendix A, "Relationships Between Homeland Security, Homeland Defense, and Defense Support of Civil Authorities."

*For further information on logistics support refer to JP 4-0, Joint Logistics.*

c. **Engineering.** Military engineering support may be required simultaneously for HD and DSCA operations. The primary focus of the engineering effort will be to sustain and assist DOD forces employed in HD. The secondary effort will be DSCA, when requested and approved IAW DOD guidance and applicable plans. The scope of engineering support for HD focuses on assured mobility, FP construction, force bed-down, geospatial information and services, and emergency stabilization and repair of damaged DOD critical infrastructure. The duration and scope of DOD engineer involvement will be directly related to the severity and magnitude of the threat, situation, or actual event. Engineer planners working either contingency or crisis action planning should develop plans with forces capable of initial tasks and priority of effort. Engineer efforts in HD may evolve into DSCA engineer actions. Whether the focus is HD or DSCA, engineering missions may require the use of Active Component (AC), RC, and contractor assets.

*For additional information on engineer organizations and assets of Services, see JP 3-34, Joint Engineer Operations.*

d. **Environmental Considerations.** Military commanders are responsible for employing environmentally responsible practices that minimize adverse impacts to human health and the environment. During all operations, strategies will be developed to reduce or eliminate negative impacts on the environment and to minimize negative impacts to mission accomplishment caused by environmental degradation. Contingency planning for HD must include environmental considerations in planning and executing operations. Operational alternatives that minimize damage to the natural environment or cultural/historic resources must be considered. HD actions undertaken during crisis are considered emergency actions, whereby national security and protection of life or property are at risk. HD response in crisis circumstances may make it necessary to take immediate actions without preparing the normal environmental planning documents; however, compliance with applicable federal, state, tribal and local laws during crisis circumstances is still a DOD goal to the maximum extent possible. Commands will initiate actions to curtail further environmental damage and to resolve environmental impacts.

*For additional information on environmental considerations, see JP 3-34, Joint Engineer Operations.*

e. **Mortuary Affairs.** GCCs are responsible for coordinating mortuary affairs (MA) operations within their AORs. DOD may be required to provide MA for HD incidents as directed by the President or when consistent with military readiness and appropriate under the circumstances and the law to support civilian entities following an incident. The NRF provides affected jurisdictions access to several federal assets relating to assist with search, recovery, evacuation, tentative identification, and internment. In HD incidents, local, state, or tribal medical examiners or coroners will usually maintain jurisdiction over both military and civilian fatalities, unless the Armed Forces Medical Examiner requests and receives jurisdiction. Jurisdiction varies depending on geographic area and is dependent on federal, state, or local laws.

*See JP 4-06,* Mortuary Affairs, *for details on employment of DOD MA assets in DSCA, mass-fatality management, CBRN CM, and HD operations.*

f. **Religious Support (RS).** Chaplains support military forces conducting HD as part of a religious support team (RST). The RSTs normally consists of at least one chaplain and an enlisted assistant of the same Service. RSTs will follow Service policy, command direction, joint and Service doctrine, and legal counsel regarding permissible chaplain activities. When directed by their unit commander after assessment of the impact of additional duties on the religious program of the unit, chaplains may assist other commands. The primary role of RSTs in emergency response is to support authorized military personnel delivering the response. RSTs normally do not provide RS to persons unaffiliated with the Services absent explicit tasking from proper command authority. However, incidental support may be provided to persons not affiliated with the Services during the execution of an authorized mission when the specific criteria are met. The four pronged test found in JP 1-05, Religious Affairs in Joint Operations, should be applied when attempting to determine who should be authorized service. Should the commander determine that emergency ministry is to be delivered to civilians, it should be within the boundaries established by the four-pronged test described in JP 1-05.

*See JP 1-05,* Religious Affairs in Joint Operations, *for details.*

g. **Health Services.** The goal of health services for HD is to minimize disease, nonbattle injuries, and battlefield injuries in order to support mission accomplishment. Health services offers overlapping care capabilities that enhance performance in a military force. These capabilities circumscribe the entirety of health services. Each capability, however, has unique attributes that can be identified, improved, and applied to attain the desired well-being of the joint force.

(1) DOD coordinates, employs, and integrates medical response through the capabilities of care: first responder care; forward resuscitative care; theater hospitalization; definitive care; and en route care.

(2) The military health system will, in most cases, have a scaled response to emergencies: first under immediate response authority and mutual aid agreements with local

and state healthcare systems; then through the National Disaster Medical System; and finally through assigned missions. Types of health services missions include: immediate medical response and health services operations.

(3) DOD medical assets and organizations may also be involved in support to local and state health providers in dealing with the aftermath of a CBRN attack and other large scale casualty producing attacks. As part of HD, there may be a requirement to augment civilian medical capabilities in the handling of casualties resulting from CBRN attacks or other toxic materials release. The ability of state and local medical facilities to handle mass casualties from CBRN effects must be assessed and factored into DOD planning.

*For additional information, see JP 3-28,* Defense Support of Civil Authorities, *JP 4-02,* Health Services.

## 8. Other Activities and Efforts

a. **Arctic Region.** The overarching strategic national security objective in the Arctic is a stable and secure region where US national interests are safeguarded and the US homeland is protected. This objective is consistent with a regional policy that reflects the relatively low level of threat in a region bounded by nation states that have not only publicly committed to working within a common framework of international law and diplomatic engagement, but also demonstrated ability and commitment to doing so over the last 50 years.

(1) DOD takes responsible steps to anticipate and prepare for Arctic operations. Capabilities are reevaluated as conditions change, and gaps are addressed in order to prepare for operations in a more accessible Arctic. Key challenges include: shortfalls in ice and weather reporting and forecasting; limitations in C2; communications; computers; ISR; harsh environmental conditions; limited inventory of ice-capable vessels; and limited shore-based infrastructure. The US has a vital Arctic neighbor and partner in Canada, with its shared values and interests in the region. DOD works with the Canadian Department of National Defence to ensure common Arctic interests are addressed in a complementary manner.

(2) There are two GCCs with Arctic responsibilities: CDRUSEUCOM and CDRUSNORTHCOM, each responsible for a portion of the Arctic Ocean aligned with adjacent land boundaries, an arrangement suited to achievement of continuity of effort with key regional partners.

b. **Information Sharing**

(1) The goal of information sharing is to attain seamless access to trusted information sharing environment throughout the AOR and between CCDRs. A collaborative environment among domestic and international military and nonmilitary (i.e., LEA) HD mission partners is particularly critical to facilitating information sharing and interoperability. It provides the ability to create and share data, information, and knowledge needed to plan, execute, and assess joint force operations in support of HD, thereby enabling a commander to make decisions faster than the adversary. The speed with which

information is gained, processed (and if necessary, sanitized for required dissemination and/or sharing), and understood influences how well we engage during emerging events.

(2) Proper organization of the battle staff support structure is another way to facilitate the synchronizing and sharing of information. In an adaptive HQ model, for example, the staff reorganizes from its normal functional areas of personnel, intelligence, operations, logistics, plans, and communications, to working groups that address current operations, future operations, joint plans, joint support, and interagency coordination. The organization must also transcend culture, policy, and technical barriers to be effective.

Intentionally Blank

# APPENDIX A
## RELATIONSHIPS BETWEEN HOMELAND SECURITY, HOMELAND DEFENSE, AND DEFENSE SUPPORT OF CIVIL AUTHORITIES

### 1. General

a. **Relationships between HS, HD, and DSCA.** Perhaps one of the greatest challenges for a military staff is operating in or near the homeland and being subject to the inherent legal and jurisdictional responsibilities that accompany such operations. This challenge is set against the evolving range of threats to the homeland–to countering transnational organizations and individual actors of concern internal and external to the US. This appendix provides additional context and considerations for the JFC and military staffs that plan and execute HD and DSCA missions. Those missions could be conducted in a simultaneous, near-simultaneous, or sequential fashion, across the threat spectrum, within or near the homeland. A full range of threats and hazards confronts the homeland. Many threats may not require a DOD-led response, and may not require a response from more than one civilian department or agency. The characterization of a particular threat, and the designated response agencies and modes, ultimately rests with the President. To prepare for wide-ranging contingencies, the USG has developed specific protocols and response options that address the coordination, integration, and responsibilities of the federal agencies to respond to the full spectrum of threats and hazards. Codification of these strategies, processes, and procedures is found in documents such as the National Strategy for Maritime Security and US Aviation Security Policy, and their respective supporting plans. These types of processes aid both the military and civil authorities to identify which agency or agencies are best suited to achieve the USG's desired outcome given the unique circumstances of the event.

b. **Homeland Security.** HS is a concerted national effort to prevent terrorist attacks within the US; reduce America's vulnerability to terrorism, major disasters, and other emergencies; and minimize the damage and recover from attacks, major disasters, and other emergencies that occur. DOD is a key part of HS, conducting HD and DSCA. DHS will usually be the federal agency with lead responsibility, and will be supported by other USG departments and agencies when requested. DOJ has lead responsibility for criminal investigations of terrorist acts or terrorist threats by individuals or groups inside the United State, or directed at US citizens or institutions abroad, where such acts are within federal criminal jurisdiction of the US, as well as for the related intelligence collection activities within the US, subject to the National Security Act of 1947 and other applicable law. The National Strategy for HS addresses the terrorist threat and provides a comprehensive framework for organizing the efforts of federal, state, local, tribal, and private organizations whose primary functions are often unrelated to national security. HD efforts often complement HS efforts and the reverse is also true.

c. **Department of Defense.** DOD protects the homeland through two distinct but interrelated missions, HD and DSCA. DOD is the federal agency with lead responsibility for HD, which may be executed by DOD alone (e.g., BMD) or include support from other USG departments and agencies. DOD's role in the DSCA mission consists of support to US civil authorities (DHS or other department or agency) for domestic emergencies and for designated LE and other activities. While these missions are distinct, some department roles and responsibilities overlap and operations require extensive coordination between lead and supporting agencies. Figure A-1 illustrates a notional relationship between HD, DSCA, and HS lead and supporting relationships and provides examples of the types of operations that can take place for each mission. HD and DSCA operations may occur in parallel and require extensive integration and synchronization. Understanding the roles and responsibilities of AC and RC forces and how they are used and the various duty statuses used to employ NG forces (Title 10 and Title 32, USC, and state active duty), is critical to achieve integration and synchronization.

d. In addition, operations may also transition from HD to DSCA to HS or vice versa (e.g., maritime security) with the lead depending on the situation and USG's desired outcome **(annotated by the arrow in Figure A-1). While the lead may transition, a single agency will always have the lead at any given time for a particular activity.** However, in the

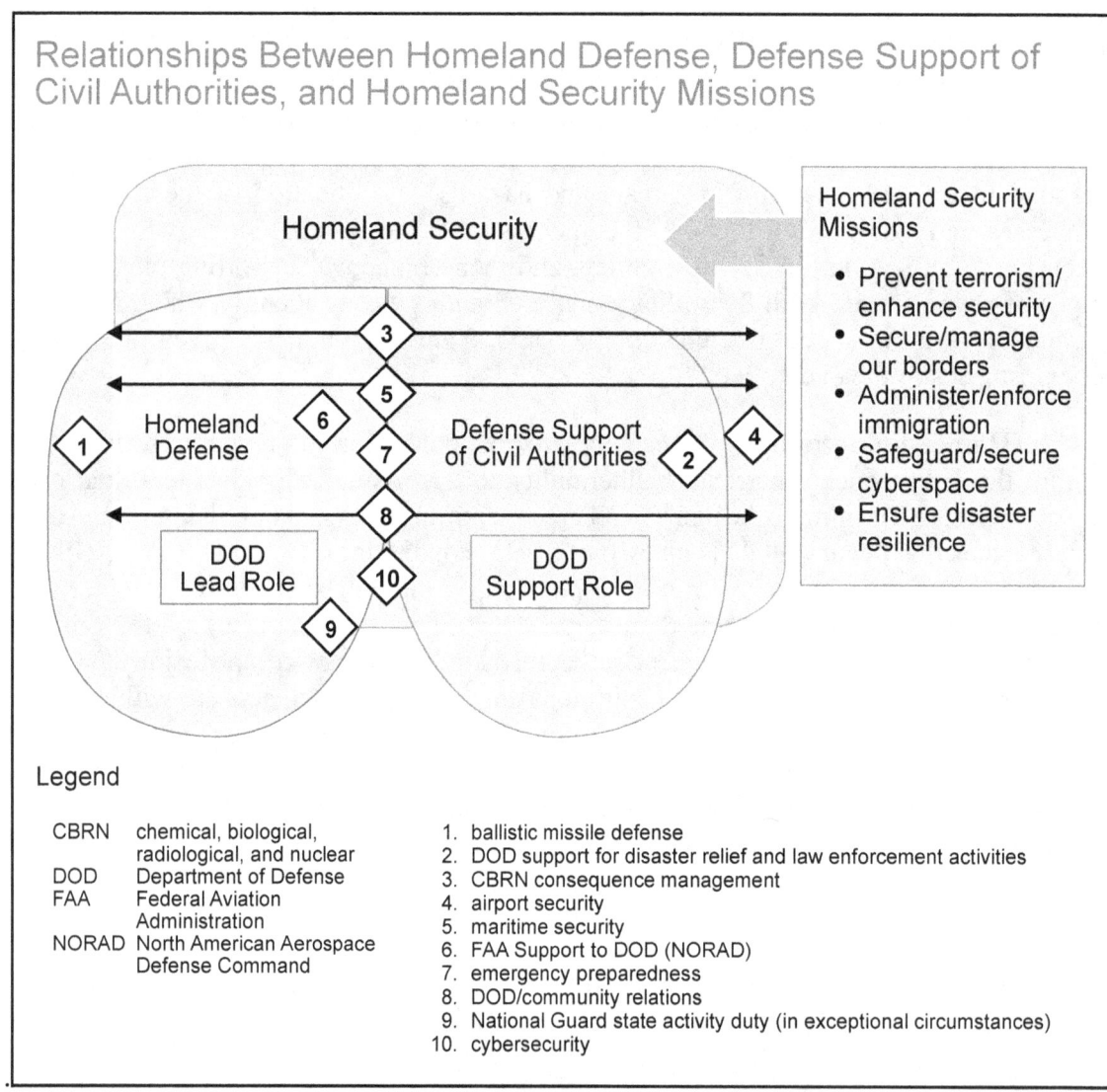

**Figure A-1. Relationships Between Homeland Defense, Defense Support of Civil Authorities, and Homeland Security Missions**

areas of overlapping responsibility, the designation of federal agency with lead responsibility may not be predetermined. In time-critical situations, on-scene leaders are empowered to conduct appropriate operations in response to a particular threat. The MOTR protocols provide guidance for maritime security, which can transition between HD, DSCA, or HS (see Chapter III, "Planning and Operations for Homeland Defense"). The NG and the reserves also play a vital role in the defense of the homeland. Figure A-1 depicts NG Title 10, USC, authorities for HD and DSCA under DOD C2 showing that the NG can conduct HD and DSCA under Title 10, USC. It also depicts NG Title 32, USC, authorities for HS, HD activities and DSCA, showing that these may be accomplished under Title 32, USC. Figure A-1 also depicts the fact that in exceptional circumstances NG forces may perform HD activities in state active duty. Title 32, USC, and state active duty fall under state or territory C2. EP remains part of DOD's overall preparedness activities. It spans HD, DSCA, and HS and includes DOD's lead, support, and enable functions. Mobile command centers and DOD aviation support to the US Secret Service are just two examples of how DOD prepares for and supports EP operations.

## 2. Command and Control Options for Transition

a. In DOD, integration includes the synchronized transfer of units into an operational commander's force prior to mission execution. HD operations require special attention regarding integration, since the C2 possibilities are extensive. Traditional considerations for integration are generally adequate when DOD is the lead and is defending against traditional external threats/aggression. However, when DOD is simultaneously performing HD operations and supporting DHS or other federal agencies, C2 becomes more complex. To promote seamless and interoperable interagency communications for the DSCA portion of DOD missions, DODI 6055.17, *DOD Installation Emergency Management (IEM) Program,* directs that DOD installations shall have a well-defined communication plan that includes the capability to communicate within the DOD, with personnel engaged in the response, as well as with civil authorities. For interoperability, the Incident Command System per the National Incident Management System will be used in the civil sector. This approach provides for common interaction when DOD is in support of civil authorities and requires planning consideration by the JFC performing such dual mission sets.

b. CCDRs cannot predict when an HD operation will transition to DSCA or vice versa. Additionally, CCDRs may need to execute HD and DSCA simultaneously. Thus, C2 in support of HD and DSCA operations should have a straightforward C2 template that permits the CCDR to respond as the supported commander, supporting commander, or both. Recent changes in law and DOD policy have increased the CCDR's C2 options. Options include using a standing JTF HQ, augmenting a core Service component HQ, or forming an ad hoc organization from various contributors. Regardless of the organizational structure, there are fundamental rules for forming and operating a JTF.

## 3. Planning Considerations for Transition

a. **Employment of RC Forces.** The RC possess resources (personnel, equipment, and skills) that can be appropriately leveraged and effectively integrated into DOD's HD plans and operations, based on the operational requirements and the capabilities of the RC. When mobilized, the United States Army Reserve, USN Reserve, United States Air Force Reserve, United States Marine Corps Reserve, ANG, ARNG, and the USCG reserve operate as active duty forces. While the NG normally is employed in Title 10, USC, status in support of HD missions, Title 32, USC, Section 902, authorizes SecDef to provide funds to state governors for NG forces to perform specified HD "activities" without first activating these forces under Title 10, USC, status. When placed on federal active duty, all RC forces conduct HD operations under Title 10, USC, guidelines.

b. **Geographic Coordinate System.** Federal, state, regional, local, and urban governmental entities use a variety of state and local grid systems and methodologies for specifying geographic locations. Latitude and longitude values can be based on different geodetic systems, or datums, the most common being World Geodetic System 1984, a global datum used by all Global Positioning System (GPS) equipment. Other datums are significant because they were chosen by a cartographical organization as the best method for representing their region and is used on printed maps and charts. The latitude and longitude on a printed map or chart may not be the same as the GPS receiver. Coordinates from the mapping system can sometimes be roughly changed into another datum using a translation. This need for translation may complicate coordinating activities between federal, state, tribal, and local responders.

c. **United States Coast Guard.** USCG is a maritime, military, multi-mission service unique among the US military branches for having a maritime LE mission (with jurisdiction in both domestic and international waters) and a federal regulatory agency mission as part of its mission set. It operates under the DHS during peacetime, and can be transferred to the Department of the Navy by the President at any time or by Congress during time of war. The USCG plays a vital role in the overall maritime defense of the homeland and is a key player in the maritime HD C2 structure pursuant to the Memorandum of Agreement Between the Department of Defense and the Department of Homeland Security for the Inclusion of the US Coast Guard in Support of Maritime Homeland Defense. Additionally, the Memorandum of Agreement between the Department of Defense and the Department of Homeland Security for Department of Defense Support to the United States Coast Guard for Maritime Homeland Security documents capabilities, roles, missions, and functions for DOD support to the USCG and facilitates the rapid transfer of DOD forces to the USCG for support of maritime HS operations. The USCG is at all times an "armed force" under Title 14, USC, and does not require Title 10, USC, authority to participate in the national defense of the US. Upon the declaration of war if Congress so directs in the declaration, or when the President directs, the USCG transfers to the Department of the Navy (Title 14, USC, Section 3). Absent such declaration or direction, the Service operates under the auspices of DHS and closely cooperates with the Navy on maritime security issues (Title 14, USC, Section 145), and assists DOD in the performance of any activity for which the USCG is especially qualified (Title 14, USC, Section 141). As the federal agency with lead responsibility for maritime HS, the USCG executes the following missions: ports, waterways, and coastal security; maritime threat response and advanced interdiction boardings; drug interdiction; migrant interdiction; defense readiness; civil maritime search and rescue, and other LE activities.

(1) As the lead for maritime HS, USCG conducts that mission IAW the Maritime Security and Response Operations Manual, both within the port and at sea.

(2) The USCG supports tactical LE operations using maritime threat response integrated force packages (IFPs) consisting of tactical LE teams, maritime safety and security teams, the maritime security response team, rotary wing air intercept assets, and supporting lift and surface assets within US ports and waterways, or well forward into the maritime approaches. IFPs conduct intercept, interdiction, and boarding operations within the context of threat response on a graduated scale. USCG assets will conduct operations while balancing risk mitigation with evidentiary necessities for further prosecution and intelligence exploitation in support of other federal agencies.

(3) Maritime security authorities which contribute both to HS and HD include domestic and international protocols and/or frameworks that coordinate partnerships, establish maritime security standards, collectively engage shared maritime security interests, and facilitate the sharing of information. Domestically, the USCG-led area maritime security committees carry out much of the maritime security regime effort. Abroad, the USCG works with individual countries and through the International Maritime Organization, a specialized agency of the United Nations.

d. **Auxiliary Organizations**

(1) **US Air Force Auxiliary.** The Air Force Auxiliary, also known as Civil Air Patrol (CAP), has forces with unique capabilities that can contribute to the successful prosecution of HD air operations. Air Education and Training Command serves as the force provider of CAP to CCDRs. CAP, a volunteer federally chartered nonprofit organization, may function as an auxiliary of the Air Force IAW Title 10, USC, Section 9442, to support Air Force noncombatant programs and missions. Such missions may include airborne surveillance and reconnaissance using visual observation and imagery, search and rescue, light airlift, or utilizing CAP aircraft as an "airborne target" during air intercept training.

(2) **USCG Auxiliary.** The USCG Auxiliary was established by Congress in 1939 under Title 14, USC. Its three missions are as follows: promote and improve recreational boating safety; support Coast Guard maritime HS efforts; and support the Coast Guard's operational, administrative, and logistical requirements.

e. **State Defense Forces.** The National Strategy for HS assigns to the states and localities the primary responsibility for funding, preparing, and operating the emergency services in the event of a terrorist attack. Given the dual-apportioned character of the NG, some see the state defense forces as the ultimate guarantor to the states and territories to handle state-specific missions in the event the NG is federalized. There are active state defense forces in 20 states and the US territory of Puerto Rico. They support, assist, and augment their state's NG forces and civilian authorities such as police and fire departments.

f. **Chapter 18 (Title 10, USC, Sections 371-382).** This chapter concerns military support for civilian LEAs and provides statutory authority for specific types of military support to LE. Title 10, USC, Section 375 directs SecDef to promulgate regulations that prohibit "direct participation by a member of the Army, Navy, Air Force, or Marine Corps in a search, seizure, arrest, or other similar activity unless participation in such activity by such member is otherwise authorized by law." This guidance is currently set forth in DODI 3025.21, *Defense Support of Civilian Law Enforcement Agencies.*

g. **Insurrection (Title 10, USC, Sections 331-335).** These statutory provisions allow the President, at the request of a state governor or legislature, or unilaterally in some circumstances, to employ the armed forces to suppress insurrection against state authority, to enforce federal laws, or to suppress rebellion. When used for such HD-related purposes in the US, the designated JFC should utilize this special application knowing that the main purpose of such employment is to help restore law and order with minimal harm to the people and property and with due respect for all law-abiding citizens.

h. **Critical Infrastructure Protection.** Most infrastructure assets are inherently interconnected and part of larger integrated systems. Therefore, the removal of one asset's functionality due to an outage or attack could have devastating effects on larger infrastructure networks, causing broad service disruptions and potentially adverse regional impacts. Almost all national and defense response capabilities rely, to some extent, on commercial infrastructures. National and DCI supporting national security functions must be available when required to protect the homeland. These will include DCI assets and DIB assets, the protection of which is the responsibility of DOD. JFCs' preparations to conduct CIP, should consider those in either a HD or DSCA role or as one transitions from one to another. For example, an explosion occurs at a major dam or nuclear facility. These are considered key assets from a national perspective. With no initial determination of cause authorities suspect terrorism. National leadership makes the initial determination to deploy a QRF for HD to protect critical infrastructure due to unknown intent and for the purpose of expediency. Subsequent to QRF arrival, an assessment is made whether an external threat or terrorism caused the event. Upon such determination of threat, but if a need for security remains, the QRF would perform security in a DSCA role until sufficient numbers of other federal agency, local LE, and/or NG (Title 32, USC) can provide necessary support.

*For complete details on the DSCA mission, see JP 3-28,* Defense Support of Civil Authorities.

# APPENDIX B
## FACILITATING INTERORGANIZATIONAL COORDINATION

### 1. General

DOD leads HD missions and will be supported by other USG departments and agencies while conducting such missions. Conversely, DOD supports other agencies for DSCA missions. Events or operations that begin as HD missions may transition to a DSCA mission (nominally for management of the consequences of an incident) or evolve to a concurrent DSCA mission. This appendix identifies agencies that normally support HD missions in some fashion, notwithstanding that some may also support DSCA missions separately, concurrently or as a follow-on requirement.

### 2. Combat Support Agencies and Other Supporting Organizations

CSAs provide direct support to the CCMDs performing HD during wartime or emergency situations and are subject to evaluation by CJCS. The paragraphs below address general and specific missions, functions, and capabilities of DOD CSAs, and selected other organizations which conduct HD activities.

a. **Defense Information Systems Agency.** DISA is responsible for planning, engineering, acquiring, fielding, and supporting global net-centric solutions and operating the Defense Information System Network to serve the needs of the President, Vice President, SecDef, and the other DOD components. DISA supports national security communications requirements and functions within the following core mission areas: communications; C2 capabilities; information assurance; computing services; interoperability, testing, and standards; DOD information networks services; engineering; and acquisition. It is the Defense Infrastructure Sector Lead Agent for the DOD information networks, per DODD 3020.40, and implements and executes the DCIP requirements.

*For more information on DISA, see DODD 5105.19,* Defense Information Systems Agency (DISA), *and its home page at www.disa.mil.*

b. **Defense Intelligence Agency.** DIA provides all-source defense intelligence to prevent strategic surprise and deliver a decision advantage to warfighters, defense planners, and policymakers. DIA has military and civilian employees located worldwide and is a major producer and manager of foreign military intelligence.

(1) The Director of DIA serves as principal adviser to SecDef and to CJCS on matters of military intelligence. The Director also chairs the Military Intelligence Board that coordinates activities of the DOD portion of the IC. Moreover, the Director serves as the principal intelligence advisor to the ASD(HD&ASA) and the military commands.

(2) With respect to HD, DIA manages the DOD warning system that alerts DOD and the USG of potential threats to the nation. DIA's Directorate for Analysis, particularly

the Defense Warning Office, assesses the most likely developing threats and the high impact threats to military capabilities and to US national infrastructures upon which the military depends for stateside operations, training, and deployment.

(3) **DIA's Disruptive** Technology Innovations Partnership (DTIP) program provides HD and US infrastructure sectors with actionable information or time-sensitive intelligence assessments for correcting serious vulnerabilities. DTIP assessments prioritize vulnerabilities according to their national security impact, whether exploited by state or non-state actors. DTIP assesses and warns of the impact of potential threats stemming from innovative applications of technologies against vulnerabilities.

(4) DIA's Directorate for Measurement and Signature Intelligence (MASINT) and Technical Collection plans, enables, and conducts MASINT and technical collection training and operations in support of HD and security requirements IAW EO 12333, *United States Intelligence Activities,* and DOD 5240.1-R, *Procedures Governing the Activities of DOD Intelligence Components that Affect United States Persons.* MASINT is technically derived intelligence which, once collected, processed, and analyzed may result in the identification of targets and signatures of target sources.

(5) DIA's Defense Combating Terrorism Center is responsible for executing the intelligence component of the DOD campaign against terrorism. It provides all-source, national level terrorism intelligence analysis, warning, and enterprise integration to enable DOD CT operations, planning, and policy.

*For more information on DIA, see DODD 5105.21,* Defense Intelligence Agency (DIA). *See also, JP 2-0,* Joint Intelligence.

c. **Defense Logistics Agency.** DLA provides worldwide logistics support for the missions of the Military Departments and the CCMDs. Specifically:

(1) DLA provides logistics support to other DOD components and certain federal agencies, foreign governments, IGOs, and others as authorized.

(2) When a federally declared emergency takes place, DOD has a supporting role to the LFA. DLA must be prepared to provide support to CCDRs or other federal agencies. The agency provides support to USNORTHCOM and USPACOM in the form of an LNO at each and through a Defense Logistics Agency support team (DST) when requested. The LNO and DST, when employed, are the primary focal points for disseminating, coordinating, and tracking GCCs' issues and concerns with DLA. DLA will provide forward-deployed DSTs (as required) in the GCCs' AORs to meet real-world and contingency requirements after valid requirements are received.

*For more information regarding DLA, see JP 4-0,* Joint Logistics.

d. **National Security Agency.** NSA provides the following support:

(1) Solutions, products, and services that contribute to information assurance.

(2) SIGINT for an effective, unified organization and control of all the foreign signals collection and processing activities of the US. NSA is authorized to produce SIGINT IAW objectives, requirements, and priorities established by the Director, National Intelligence with the advice of the National Foreign Intelligence Board.

(3) Information systems security activities, as assigned by SecDef, to include managing and providing OPCON of the US SIGINT System. EO 12333, *United States Intelligence Activities,* describes the responsibilities of NSA in more detail.

e. **Defense Contract Management Agency (DCMA).** DCMA works directly with defense suppliers to help ensure that DOD, federal and allied government supplies and services are delivered on time, at projected cost, and that they meet all performance requirements. DCMA performs all contract audits for DOD and provides accounting and financial advisory services regarding contracts and subcontracts to all DOD components responsible for procurement and contract administration. Within the DCIP, DCMA (subordinate to the Under Secretary of Defense [Acquisition, Technology, and Logistics]) is DOD's lead for the DIB sector.

*For more information on DCMA, go to the DCMA webpage at www.dcma.mil.*

f. **National Geospatial-Intelligence Agency (NGA).** NGA provides timely, relevant, and accurate geospatial intelligence (GEOINT) in support of national security objectives. GEOINT is the exploitation and analysis of imagery and geospatial information to describe, assess, and visually depict physical features and geographically referenced activities on the earth. Geospatial intelligence consists of imagery, imagery intelligence, and geospatial information IAW Title 10, USC, Section 467, NGA also:

(1) Supports customers in the defense, LE, intelligence, federal, and civil communities with its analytic GEOINT capabilities.

(2) Supports DOD and civil authorities by building integrated datasets to support the COP and situational awareness. These datasets provide a common frame of reference for federal decision makers and operational planners for critical infrastructure vulnerability analysis and for domestic incident management and CIP.

(3) In concert with other federal partners, serves as the imagery and geospatial data broker, integrator, and consolidator in building a single database to support domestic situational awareness, incident management, and CIP.

(4) Provides integrated geospatial information in support of the planning and execution of HD exercises where there is federal, DOD, state, and local government participation.

(5) Deploys fully equipped geospatial analytic teams to support military and civilian exercises as well as other crisis and national special security events in real time.

(6) Provides direct, tailored, geospatial information support.

(7) Provides externally assigned support personnel as part of the NGA support team (NST) program to CCMDs, the Services, IC partners, and civilian agencies such as Department of State, FBI, and DHS. These embedded NST personnel provide day-to-day GEOINT support to the commands or agencies and have the capability to reach back to NGA for requirements that exceed the capacity or capability of the team at the command. In addition, NGA maintains a group of support personnel as part of NGA voluntary deployment teams (NVDTs) that can deploy to augment an NST. NST members or individuals from the NVDT can be called upon to participate as part of a national intelligence support team, along with other members of the IC in response to a crisis or emergency situation to augment the staffs of a joint intelligence operations center, command, or agency.

g. **Defense Threat Reduction Agency.** DTRA safeguards the US and its allies from global WMD threats by integrating, synchronizing, and providing expertise, technologies, and capabilities across all operating environments. The Director, DTRA is dual-hatted as the Director, SCC-WMD, whose mission is to synchronize CWMD efforts across our military's geographic commands and leverage the people, programs, and interagency relationships of DTRA at the strategic level. DTRA capabilities that help reduce, eliminate, and counter the WMD threat and mitigate its effects in defense of the homeland include the following:

(1) DTRA's Joint Operations Center provides 24/7 analytical support through subject matter experts for the full range of operational computational tools including targeting support, consequence assessment, mission assurance, collateral damage and effects, developmental and non-DTRA technology, and residential and mobile training.

(2) Balanced survivability assessments are mission survivability assessments of critical national or theater mission systems, networks, architectures, infrastructures, and assets of the US and its allies. Assessment areas include surveillance operations, physical security, telecommunications, IO, structural protection and response, utility subsystems, WMD protection, emergency operations, and electromagnetic protection.

(3) Consequence management advisory teams provide technical and scientific subject matter experts, planners, and hazard prediction modeling support to CCDRs and federal coordinating agencies or their delegated representatives in response to catastrophic incidents involving WMD in the US and abroad, when requested.

(4) Deployable CWMD plans teams assist CCMDs or other supported commanders with CWMD planning and analysis of existing plans, or assist the supported commander in developing plans, annexes, or appendices for CWMD operations.

(5) Joint Staff integrated vulnerability assessments provide a vulnerability-based assessment of DOD installations/facilities to provide responsible commanders with recommendations to deter, detect, and defend against terrorist events and respond, and recover from incidents of all hazards nature to include CBRN.

(6) Technical support groups located in CONUS, USPACOM, United States

European Command (USEUCOM), and US Central Command provide the capability to train, advise, assist, and equip in order to conduct tactical low-visibility radiological search operations.

h. **Joint Interagency Task Force South.** JIATF-S is a multiservice, multiagency national task force based at Naval Air Station Key West, FL. The illegal production and trafficking of drugs undermines security and stability in Latin America and the Caribbean and also threatens US national security. JIATF-S detects and monitors suspect aircraft and maritime vessels, and then provides this information to international and interagency partners who have the authority to interdict illicit shipments and arrest members of TCOs. JIATF-S brokers all parties with regard to intended targets and operations, matching capabilities with authorities. With DOD as the interagency lead agent, JIATF-S includes all five branches of the US military and USG LEAs, including the Immigrations Customs Enforcement HS Investigations, the FBI, Customs and Border Protection, and DEA. Added to this group of US agencies are the military and LE capabilities of national partners in Latin America, the Caribbean, and Europe, which include LNOs on the ground at JIATF-S' HQ, plus other countries' military and LE capabilities. In support of HD, JIATF-S helps track military equipment destined for terrorist organizations. The inter-organizational coordination that occurs on a daily basis promotes shared responsibilities and facilitates appropriate and legal LE information sharing between non-DOD LEAs (both US and other countries). This, and the combined operations that are conducted under JIATF-S auspices, support a concerted HD and HS approach to protecting US national interests in Latin America and the Caribbean.

i. **Missile Defense Agency.** The MDA is a research, development, and acquisition agency within the DOD. This includes using international cooperation by supporting mutual security interests in missile defense. The agency works with the CCDRs (e.g., USNORTHCOM, USPACOM, USSTRATCOM) to develop BMDS technologies and a program to address the challenges of an evolving threat. The MDA goal is to develop, test and prepare for deployment a missile defense system to engage all classes and ranges of ballistic missile threats. The agency uses their MDA Operations Center as the central communications node for situation monitoring and information collection on current BMDS performance and to coordinate MDA's support to the CCDRs, Services and other agencies, and provide staff assistance to BMDS element managers. The MOC functions include supporting emergency activation of BMDS test bed resources for operational execution, and for receiving and disseminating Strategic Arms Reduction Treaty and Treaty on Open Skies inspection information. MDA also supports BMDS asset management and logistical support. Asset management enables event owners and asset owners to deconflict their events and asset requirements (e.g., tests and maintenance), and to use a cooperative approach between CCDRs, Services, and MDA to provide for the sustainability and maintainability of MDA elements and components.

j. **Department of Defense Cyber Crime Center (DC3).** DC3 provides digital forensics support to the DOD and to other LEAs. The DC3's main focus is in criminal, CI, CT, and fraud investigations, but two of the groups associated with the DC3 support HD-related efforts. These are the DOD-Defense Industrial Base Collaborative Information Sharing Environment (DCISE) and the National Cyber Investigative Joint Task Force-Analytical Group (NCIJTF-AG).

(1)  DCISE is the focal point and clearinghouse for referrals of intrusion events on DIB unclassified corporate networks.  The DCISE is a collaborative operational information sharing environment among multiple partners that produces threat information products for industry partners with reciprocal responsibilities of providing notice of anomalies and sharing of relevant media.

(2)  The NCIJTF-AG coordinates with the National Cyber Investigative Joint Task Force, a cyberspace investigation coordination organization overseen by the FBI which serves as a multi-agency national focal point for coordinating, integrating, and sharing pertinent information related to cyberspace threat investigations.  The NCIJTF-AG mitigates, neutralizes, and disrupts cyberspace intrusions presenting a national security threat.  The NCIJTF-AG synthesizes a COP of hostile intrusion related activity to aid investigations, review all source data, and support timely reporting in order to shrink the cyberspace CI response time on defense-related intrusions.

3.  **Other Federal Departments, Organizations, and Agencies**

a. The Department of Homeland Security.  Figure B-1 shows the organizational structure of DHS.  Key directorates and components include:

(1) **The Science and Technology Directorate** is the primary research and development arm of DHS.  The Science and Technology Directorate provides federal, state, and local officials with the technology and capabilities to protect the homeland.

(2) **The National Protection and Programs Directorate (NPPD)** bolsters the nation's security through a multilayered system of preparedness measures based on risk assessment and management.  Working with state, local, and private sector partners, the directorate identifies threats, determines vulnerabilities, and targets resources where risk is greatest.  Through grants and training on both national and local levels, DHS fosters a layered system of protective measures to safeguard US borders, seaports, bridges and highways, and critical information systems.  NPPD has five divisions: Federal Protective Services; Office of Cybersecurity and Communications; Office of Infrastructure Protection; Office of Risk Management and Analysis; and United Sates Visitor and Immigrant Status Indicator Technology (US-VISIT) (biometrics-based technological solutions).

(3) **The Office of Policy** strengthens HS by developing and integrating Department-wide policies, planning, and programs in order to better coordinate DHS's prevention, protection, response, and recovery missions.

(4) **The Office of Health Affairs** coordinates all medical activities of DHS to ensure appropriate preparation for and response to incidents having medical significance.

(5) **The Office of Intergovernmental Affairs** promotes an integrated national approach to HS by coordinating and advancing federal interaction with state, local, tribal, and territorial governments.  It is responsible for opening HS dialogue with executive-level partners at the state, local, tribal, and territorial levels, along with the national associations that represent them.

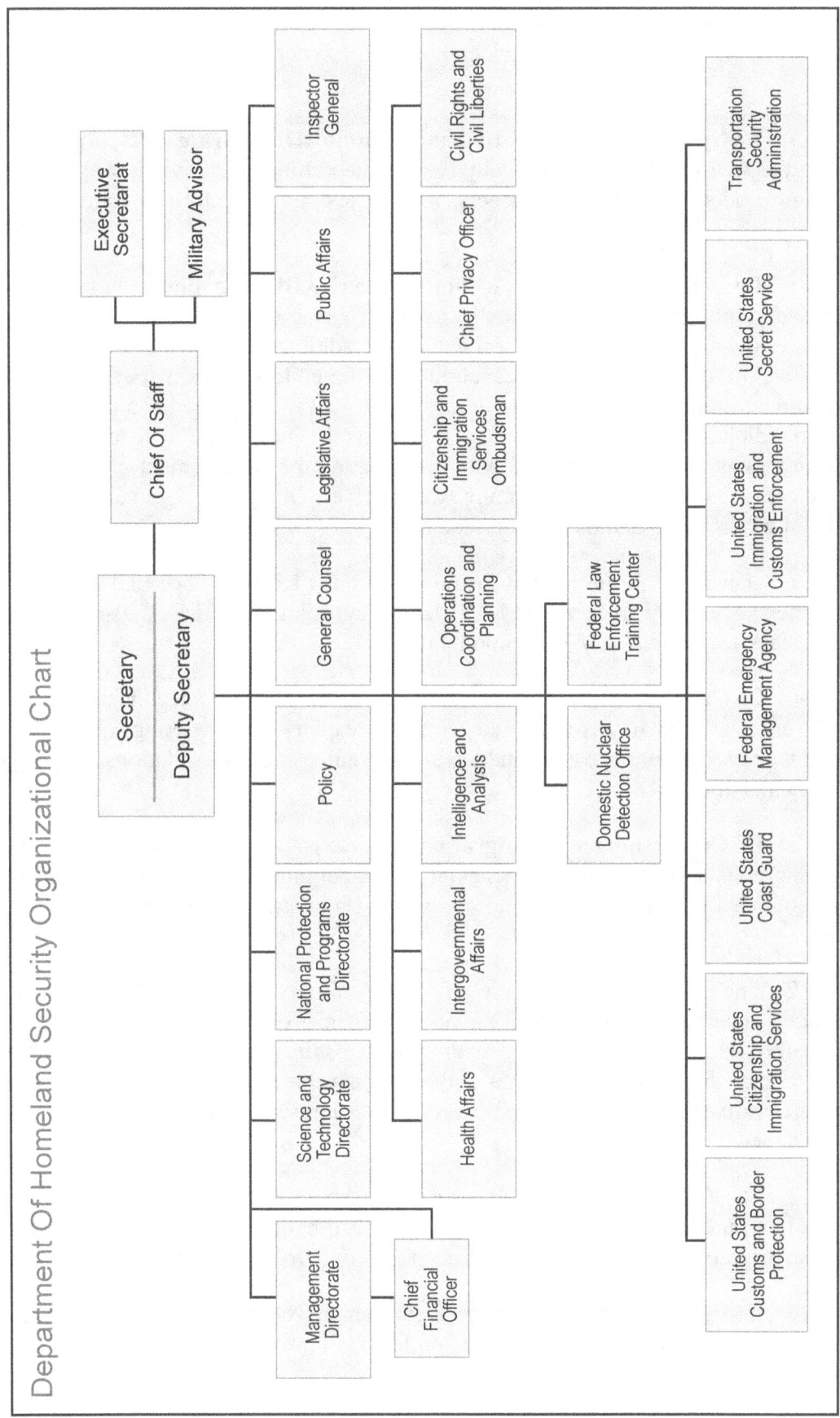

**Figure B-1. Department of Homeland Security Organizational Chart**

(6) **The Office of Intelligence and Analysis** is responsible for using information and intelligence from multiple sources to identify and assess current and future threats to the US.

(7) **The Operations Coordination and Planning Directorate** is responsible for monitoring the security of the US on a daily basis and coordinating activities within DHS and with governors, advisors, LE partners, and critical infrastructure operators areas nationwide.

(8) **The Domestic Nuclear Detection Office (DNDO)** is a jointly staffed office established to improve the Nation's capability to detect and report unauthorized attempts to import, possess, store, develop, or transport nuclear or radiological material for use against the Nation, and to further enhance this capability over time. It is the primary entity in the USG for implementing domestic nuclear detection efforts for a managed and coordinated response to radiological and nuclear threats, as well as the integration of federal nuclear forensics programs. DNDO is charged with coordinating the development of the global nuclear detection and reporting architecture, with partners from federal, state, local, and international governments and the private sector.

(9) **Federal Law Enforcement Training Center (FLETC).** The FLETC serves as an interagency LE training organization for 91 federal agencies. The FLETC also provides services to state, local, tribal, and international LEAs.

(10) **US Customs and Border Protection** is responsible for protecting the nation's borders in order to prevent terrorists and terrorist weapons from entering the US and facilitating the flow of legitimate trade and travel while enforcing US regulations, including immigration and drug laws.

(11) **US Citizenship and Immigration Services** is the USG agency that oversees lawful immigration to the US. It is responsible for the administration of immigration and naturalization adjudication functions, and establishing immigration services policies and priorities.

(12) **The US Coast Guard** is one of the five military Services of the US and the only military organization within DHS. The USCG missions encompass three areas: maritime safety, maritime security, and maritime stewardship. The USCG is an adaptable, responsive military force whose broad legal authorities, capable assets, geographic diversity, and expansive partnerships provide a persistent presence along US rivers, in the ports, littoral regions, and the high seas.

(13) **The Federal Emergency Management Agency** supports US citizens and first responders to ensure that as a nation we work together to build, sustain, and improve our capability to prepare for, protect against, respond to, recover from, and mitigate all hazards.

(14) **US Immigration and Customs Enforcement** promotes HS and public safety through the criminal and civil enforcement of federal laws governing border control,

customs, trade, and immigration. It is responsible for identifying and shutting down vulnerabilities on the nation's border, and in the economic, transportation and infrastructure security.

(15) **The US Secret Service** mission is to safeguard the nation's financial infrastructure and payment systems to preserve the integrity of the economy, and to protect the President and other national leaders, visiting heads of state and government, designated sites and national special security events. The Secret Service's partnerships—public and private, domestic and international, LE and civilian—play a critical role in preventing, detecting, investigating, and mitigating the effects of electronic and financial crimes.

(16) **TSA** protects the nation's transportation systems to ensure freedom of movement for people and commerce.

*For additional information on DHS directorates and offices, refer to JP 3-08,* Interorganizational Coordination During Joint Operations.

b. **Department of Justice/Federal Bureau of Investigation.** As the lead for crisis management and CT, the Attorney General has responsibility for investigating terrorist acts or threats, coordinating LE activities to detect, prevent, preempt and disrupt terrorist attacks, and, if an attack occurs, to identify and prosecute the perpetrators. DOJ has charged the FBI with executing its lead agency responsibilities for managing a federal LE response to threats or acts of terrorism that take place within US territory or those occurring in international waters that do not involve flag vessels of foreign countries. The FBI maintains two operational watches within a single operations center, the Strategic Information and Operations Center (SIOC) Watch and CT Watch. The SIOC Watch retains primary daily responsibility for criminal investigative matters, administrative issues, and information management. The CT Watch works side-by-side with the SIOC Watch to support seamless and efficient handling of strategic information and emerging events, both domestically and globally. The dual location of both watches supports the proper flow of information to FBI HQ, field divisions, legal attachés, and other government agency operations centers within the IC. The Crisis Coordination and Administration Unit within the SIOC coordinates and prepares the operational activation system at FBI HQ for a watch, threat or incident, special event, or natural disaster. This includes coordination with field offices, legal attachés, and specialized national assets when required to manage a critical incident. Additionally, the SIOC supports Bureau field commanders who represent the FBI worldwide in major investigations, tactical operations, and other matters.

c. **Department of Energy (DOE).** DOE/National Nuclear Security Administration (NNSA) is the USG's primary capability for radiological and nuclear emergency response and for providing security to the nation from nuclear terrorism. DOE maintains a high level of readiness for protecting and serving the US and its allies through the development, implementation, and coordination of programs and systems designed to respond in the event of a nuclear terrorist incident or other types of radiological accidents. DOE provides a dedicated resource capable of responding rapidly to nuclear or radiological incidents worldwide. Key areas include: radiological search teams to locate and identify radiological material; render safe capability to make sure a nuclear device is safe; and CBRN CM response to determine the spread of radiological material.

(1) DOE also has a variety of emergency response assets. These assets encompass four core competencies: core knowledge of US nuclear weapons, "dirty bombs" and crude nuclear devices; core knowledge of use and interpretation of specialized radiation detection equipment; core technical operations; and core technical support requirements.

(2) The assets are:

(a) **Aerial Measuring System (AMS).** AMS characterizes ground-deposited radiation from aerial platforms. These platforms include fixed wing and rotary wing aircraft with radiological measuring equipment, computer analysis of aerial measurements, and equipment to locate lost radioactive sources, conduct aerial surveys, or map large areas of contamination.

(b) **Accident Response Group (ARG).** The ARG response element is comprised of scientists, technical specialists, crisis managers, and equipment ready for short-notice dispatch to the scene of a US nuclear weapon accident.

(c) **National Atmospheric Release Advisory Center (NARAC).** NARAC is a computer based EP and response predictive capability. NARAC provides real-time computer predictions of the atmospheric transport of material from radioactive release.

(d) **Federal Radiological Monitoring and Assessment Center (FRMAC).** FRMAC is an interagency federal asset available on request by the DHS and state and local agencies to respond to a nuclear or radiological incident. The FRMAC is an interagency organization with representation from the NNSA, DOD, the Environmental Protection Agency, the Department of Health and Human Services, FBI, and other federal agencies.

(e) **Radiological Assistance Program (RAP).** RAP also provides advice and radiological assistance for incidents involving radioactive materials that pose a threat to the public health and safety or the environment. RAP can provide field deployable teams of health physics professionals equipped to conduct radiological search, monitoring, and assessment activities.

(f) **Radiation Emergency Assistance Center/Training Site (REAC/TS).** REAC/TS provides medical advice, specialized training, and onsite assistance for the treatment of radiation exposure accidents.

(g) **Nuclear Emergency Support Team (NEST).** NEST provides technical assistance to a LFA to deal with nuclear threats and incidents. NEST addresses threats by domestic and foreign terrorists that may have the will and means to employ WMD. NEST assists in the identification, characterization, rendering safe and final disposition of any nuclear weapon or radioactive device.

d. **Department of Transportation/Federal Aviation Administration.** The mission of DOT is to serve the US by ensuring a fast, safe, efficient, accessible, and convenient transportation system that meets our vital national interests and enhances the quality of life of the American people. Under DOT, the FAA provides air movement and flight plan data for all commercial and other aircraft operations that are critically important in determining if any aircraft are deviating from normal planned flight operations. The FAA oversees the safety of civil aviation and maintains primary jurisdiction over all air space within the US National Airspace System. In close coordination with DOD and NORAD, FAA clears air traffic as needed to expedite intercept operations. The safety mission of the FAA is first and foremost and includes the issuance and enforcement of regulations and standards related to the manufacture, operation, certification, and maintenance of aircraft. The agency is responsible for the rating and certification of airmen and for certification of airports serving air carriers. It also regulates a program to protect the security of civil aviation, and enforces regulations under the Hazardous Materials Transportation Act for shipments by air. The FAA, which operates a network of airport towers, air route traffic control centers, and flight service stations, develops air traffic rules, allocates the use of airspace, and provides for the security control of air traffic to meet national defense requirements. Other responsibilities include maintaining most of the radars which perform air surveillance over the CONUS FAA control centers, providing cueing for targets of interest, and providing maintenance and logistics support for nearly all ground to air radios used by the air defense sectors (ADSs). These and other support activities and procedures are governed by a series of agreements and FAA orders.

e. **National Counterterrorism Center (NCTC).** The NCTC is organizationally part of the Office of the Director of National Intelligence and is staffed by more than 500 personnel, approximately 60 percent of whom are detailed to NCTC from more than 16 departments and agencies. NCTC has two core missions. The first is to serve as the primary organization in the USG for analysis and integration of all terrorism intelligence, and in that capacity the director reports to the Director of National Intelligence. The second mission is to conduct strategic operational planning for CT activities integrating all elements of US national power. In this role, the director reports to the President. The NCTC serves as the central and shared knowledge bank on terrorism information, provides all-source intelligence support to government-wide CT activities, and establishes the IT systems and architectures within the NCTC and between the NCTC and other agencies that enable access to, as well as integration, dissemination, and use of, terrorism information. One way the NCTC supports HD is its operation of a secure website, NCTC Online CURRENT, which serves as the primary dissemination mechanism for terrorism information produced by the NCTC and other CT mission partners, to include international partners. NCTC Online CURRENT is directly available to a broad audience to include USG partners with an operational focus such as the FBI's joint terrorism task forces and DOD's CCMDs.

f. **Centers for Disease Control and Prevention (CDC).** The CDC is a US federal agency under the Department of Health and Human Services. The CDC is the US' national level public health institute and works to protect public health and safety by providing information to enhance health decisions, and it promotes health through partnerships with state health departments and other organizations.

Intentionally Blank

# APPENDIX C
## NORTH AMERICAN AEROSPACE DEFENSE COMMAND MISSIONS, ORGANIZATION, AND STRUCTURE

> *"NORAD is the cornerstone of our air defense capability. Our air defense success rests on an integrated system for air surveillance and defense against air threats at all altitudes."*
>
> **Strategy for Homeland Defense and Civil Support**
> **June 2005**

## 1. North American Aerospace Defense Command Overview

a. Since 1957, Canada and the US have defended the skies of North America. A formal NORAD Agreement between the two governments was signed on 12 May 1958 to establish NORAD as a bi-national command. Using data from satellites, as well as airborne and ground-based radars, NORAD monitors, validates, and warns of attack against the Canadian and US homelands by aircraft, missiles, and space vehicles against both symmetric as well as asymmetric threats. The command ensures Canadian and US air sovereignty through a network of alert fighters, tankers, airborne early warning aircraft, and ground-based air defense assets cued by military and interagency surveillance radars, such as those of the FAA and its Canadian equivalent, NAV CANADA.

b. As an executed international covenant, the NORAD Agreement is binding under international law. The CDS and the US CJCS provide the Terms of Reference to the NORAD Agreement to supplement and clarify military responsibilities directed or implied by the agreement.

c. In the context of NORAD's missions, "North America" means Alaska, Canada, the CONUS, Puerto Rico and the US Virgin Islands, to include the Air Defense Identification Zone, the air approaches, maritime approaches and territorial seas, and the internal navigable waterways (principally the Gulf of St. Lawrence, St. Lawrence Seaway System, Great Lakes, and other internal waterways of concern as identified by CDRNORAD). Responsibility for aerospace warning and aerospace control of US territory outside North America (e.g., Hawaii and Guam) lies with the appropriate GCC.

**The 2006 North American Aerospace Defense Command (NORAD) Agreement Established Three Primary Missions For NORAD:**

**1. Aerospace Warning for North America.**

**2. Aerospace Control for North America.**

**3. Maritime Warning for North America.**

## 2. Missions

a. **Aerospace warning** consists of processing, assessing, and disseminating intelligence and information related to man-made objects in the air and space domains, plus the detection, validation, and warning of attack against North America whether by aircraft, missiles or space vehicles, utilizing mutual support arrangements with other commands and agencies. An integral part of aerospace warning entails monitoring of global aerospace activities and related developments. NORAD's aerospace warning mission for North America includes support of US commands that are responsible for missile defense.

b. **Aerospace control** consists of providing surveillance and exercising OPCON of the airspace of the US and Canada. OPCON is defined in the NORAD Agreement and NORAD Terms of Reference as the authority to direct, coordinate, and control the operational activities of forces assigned, attached, or otherwise made available to NORAD. Aerospace control involves a continuum of combined air operations that includes air sovereignty operations aimed at controlling access to the sovereign airspace of North America, air enforcement operations aimed at controlling activities approaching or within sovereign airspace, and air defense operations aimed at defending against air attack. This means that NORAD has the authority to monitor, control, and prosecute (in cooperation with the FAA and Transport Canada/NAV CANADA) all unwanted and unauthorized activity approaching and/or operating within North American airspace, including cross-border air operations.

c. **Maritime warning** consists of processing, assessing, and disseminating intelligence and information related to the respective maritime approaches to the US and Canada. It also includes warning of maritime threats to, or attacks against North America utilizing mutual support arrangements with other commands and agencies, to enable identification, validation, and response by national commanders and agencies responsible for maritime defense and security. These tasks develop a comprehensive shared understanding of maritime activities to better identify potential maritime threats to North American security. Maritime surveillance and control shall continue to be exercised by national commands and, as appropriate, coordinated bilaterally.

## 3. Supporting Mission Areas and Systems

a. **Integrated Tactical Warning and Attack Assessment.** Tactical warning is a warning after initiation of a strategic or tactical aerospace threat event based on an evaluation of information from all available sources. Attack assessment is an evaluation of information to determine the potential or actual nature and objectives of an attack for the purpose of providing information for timely decisions. The ITW/AA system is a critical component of the US nuclear C2 system and is comprised of the sensors, command centers, and communications networks required to detect, assess, and communicate its information to designated users. **The main purpose of the ITW/AA system is to provide timely, reliable, and unambiguous warning information of ballistic missile, space, and air attacks on North America.** To provide ITW/AA of an aerospace attack on North America, NORAD, as a supported command, correlates and integrates relevant information. Space surveillance, nuclear detonation detection, and ballistic missile warning information is provided by USSTRATCOM for NORAD to execute its aerospace warning mission for North America.

CDRUSSTRATCOM, as a supporting commander, retains OPCON over USSTRATCOM-assigned ballistic missile and space surveillance and warning systems, the Nuclear Detonation Detection System, and command, control and communications systems. CDRNORAD retains the authority to redirect operational priorities of the ITW/AA systems to execute NORAD assigned missions IAW the priority assigned to attacks against North America.

b. **Routine Air Operations.** NORAD is responsible for providing surveillance and control of North American airspace. This includes:

(1) Day-to-day surveillance and control of the airspace approaches to and the airspace within North America to safeguard the sovereign airspace of both Canada and the US.

(2) Surveillance and control includes the capability to detect, identify, monitor, and, if necessary, take appropriate actions (ranging from visual identification to destruction) against manned or unmanned air-breathing vehicles approaching North America.

(3) Air defense against manned or unmanned air-breathing weapon systems attacking North America.

c. **Information and Intelligence Sharing.** NORAD aerospace warning, maritime warning, and aerospace control missions require effective information and intelligence sharing by many organizations and agencies within Canada and the US. A "need to share" philosophy facilitates the effective execution of these NORAD missions on behalf of the governments of Canada and the US.

d. **Interagency Cooperation.** The effective execution of NORAD missions requires significant cooperation with agencies outside the Department of National Defence in Canada and the DOD in the US. NORAD is authorized direct liaison with these agencies in order to solicit and acquire the necessary cooperation, while keeping appropriate national commands and authorities informed.

e. **Direct Communications.** CDRNORAD is authorized direct communications with the CDS, CJCS, and SecDef, and with Commander, Canada Joint Operations Command (CJOC), CDRUSNORTHCOM, CDRUSPACOM, CDRUSSTRATCOM, CDRUSSOUTHCOM, nation Service chiefs, and other commanders on matters relative to NORAD's missions. This includes requests to appropriate agencies to expedite the release of classified information to facilitate the accomplishment of NORAD's missions.

*"Close cooperation, liaison, and intelligence and information sharing among these commands will ensure the ability of our armed forces to act, in a timely and coordinated fashion, to deter, identify, disrupt and defeat threats to Canada and the United States."*

**Canada-United States (CANUS) Basic Defense Document**
**July 2006**

f. **Counterdrug (CD) Operations.** The aerial and maritime transit of illegal drugs into North America has been identified as a threat to the national security of Canada and the US by both governments. To counter this threat, the 1989 National Defense Authorization Act assigned DOD as the federal agency with lead responsibility in the detection and monitoring of illegal airborne and maritime drug trafficking into the US. To accomplish this mission, SecDef tasked CDRNORAD and selected CCDRs to conduct detection and monitoring operations. Likewise, the Canadian National Drug Strategy named the Canadian National Defense Headquarters (NDHQ) as a supporting department to the Royal Canadian Mounted Police. As a result, 1 Canadian Air Division (CAD) is responsible for conducting CD operations when directed by NDHQ. To accomplish this mission, NORAD conducts operations to detect and monitor aerial transit of drug trafficking into North America; coordinates with other federal, provincial, state and local agencies engaged in detecting, monitoring and apprehending aerial drug traffic, and integrates NORAD operations into an effective CD network.

*It is important to understand the differences between Canadian and US law for military support to LEAs. NORAD Instruction 10-24 provides additional detail on this subject and should be consulted by those planning or executing CD activities for NORAD.*

### 4. North American Aerospace Defense Command Organization

NORAD is organized on three distinct levels. The HQ NORAD staff and the Command Center operate at the **"strategic"** level. The three NORAD regions conduct activities at the "operational" level and the ADSs and their TACON forces operate at the **"tactical"** level.

a. Missions are accomplished through a combination of assigned and attached Canadian and US forces (AC, NG, and reserves). These forces are employed in three NORAD regions, further described in paragraph 6, "North American Aerospace Defense Command Subordinate Commands."

b. **Commander NORAD.** CDRNORAD and the Deputy Commander cannot be from the same country, and their appointments must be approved by both Canadian and USGs. The jurisdiction of CDRNORAD over those forces specifically made available to NORAD by the two governments is limited to "OPCON."

c. **Commander, United States Element North American Aerospace Defense Command (CDRUSELEMNORAD).** This officer is the senior US officer assigned to NORAD. United States Element North American Aerospace Defense Command (USELEMNORAD) serves as an administrative construct to permit the assignment or attachment of US forces to perform NORAD missions. Global Force Management Implementation Guidance Section II, Assignment of Forces (Forces for Unified Commands) states, "Although not a CCDR, CDRUSELEMNORAD, exercises COCOM over US forces made available to NORAD."

d. **Headquarters, NORAD.** HQ NORAD provides the strategic guidance necessary for the regions to execute their assigned missions. Additionally, the HQ coordinates with the senior military staffs of both countries as well as other CCDRs who may be in a supporting role. HQ NORAD and the command centers must be composed of integrated staffs with representatives of both countries.

e. **Headquarters, NORAD Staff Organization.** The HQ NORAD staff is organized along the same J-code construct as the Joint Staff. In addition, the commander's staff includes Canadian and US political advisors, an interagency group, a Washington Office, and special assistants for NG and reserve affairs. A unique aspect of the HQ NORAD staff is that all these staff elements are "dual-hatted" as both NORAD and USNORTHCOM organizations, with the exception of the operations directorate, which is a NORAD-only organization. Despite the majority of the staff being "dual-hatted" with USNORTHCOM, the commands remain separate with complementary missions, roles and responsibilities.

5. **North American Aerospace Defense Command Relations with Other Commands**

a. **United States Northern Command.** NORAD and USNORTHCOM share a special and unique relationship. A majority of USNORTHCOM's AOR and NORAD's OA overlap. Note that in the NORAD Agreement this is normally referred to as an AO. Each command has its missions defined by separate sources. NORAD is a bi-national military organization which exists under the authority of the North Atlantic Treaty, the NORAD Agreement, the NORAD Terms of Reference, and the Canada-United States (CANUS) Basic Defense Document (CANUS BDD) between Canada and the US. Conversely, USNORTHCOM is a purely US military organization based on the US UCP. USNORTHCOM forces operating in the same area as NORAD forces may provide tactical intercept information to NORAD forces. Conversely, NORAD air defense control assets may provide tactical intercept information to USNORTHCOM forces while they remain under the OPCON of their respective commander. To achieve combined effects, USNORTHCOM accomplishes coordination with numerous commands and agencies. For instance:

(1) USNORTHCOM is responsible for planning, organizing, and as directed, for executing HD operations within the USNORTHCOM AOR in concert with missions performed by NORAD. The mission and geographic overlaps between NORAD and USNORTHCOM require both commands to coordinate and synchronize their operations.

(2) USNORTHCOM coordinates with NORAD for the ground defense of Alaska.

(3) USNORTHCOM coordinates with NORAD and CJOC for the ground defense of CONUS.

(4) In conjunction with the Canadian Chief of Maritime Staff, USNORTHCOM coordinates with NORAD for the defense of maritime approaches to North America including air defense coordination.

(5) USNORTHCOM coordinates air defense operations with NORAD.

(6) To facilitate coordination, a Memorandum of Understanding Between North American Aerospace Defense Command and United States Northern Command and Canada Command Concerning the Exchange of Information Between the Three Commands of

Commander's Critical Information Requirements and Other Information Requirements, was codified on 25 January 2012.

b. **United States Strategic Command** . USSTRATCOM support to NORAD includes the following:

(1) Provide the missile warning and space surveillance information necessary to fulfill the US commitment to the NORAD Agreement.

(2) Provide ITW/AA of space, missile, and air attacks on CONUS and Alaska if NORAD becomes unable to accomplish the aerospace warning mission.

(3) Coordinate with NORAD to support accomplishments of both commands' missions during crisis and war.

c. **United States Transportation Command.** USTRANSCOM provides common-user and commercial air, land, and sea transportation, terminal management and aerial refueling to support the global deployment, employment, sustainment, and redeployment of US forces. As such, USTRANSCOM is responsible for the following support to NORAD:

(1) Provide air-refueling support to NORAD as required. Ensure main and forward operating bases are capable of supporting designated refueling and associated support operations.

(2) Support NORAD deployment, resupply, and redeployment with air, sea, and other assets, as directed by SecDef.

(3) Coordinate force movement requirements and related materials (including strategic aeromedical evacuation) involving common user lift.

d. **United States Pacific Command (USPACOM).** USPACOM is responsible for planning, organizing, and as directed executing HD operations within the USPACOM AOR. The mission and geographic proximity between NORAD and USPACOM require both commands to coordinate and synchronize their operations.

e. **United States European Command.** USEUCOM's AOR extends across the Atlantic Ocean to the west coast of Greenland and east to approximately 45 degrees West Longitude. NORAD's OA and USEUCOM's AOR overlap.

f. **United States Southern Command.** NORAD's OA and USSOUTHCOM's AOR overlap. NORAD has a memorandum of understanding (MOU) with USSOUTHCOM to address issues of mutual concern, to list support rendered by one party to the other and to deconflict their operations when necessary. Of particular interest to NORAD, this MOU addresses CD operations and US military operations in the vicinity of Cuba.

g. **North American Aerospace Defense Command, CJOC, and US Northern Command.** NORAD supports CJOC and USNORTHCOM in their assigned missions to defend Canada and the US. NORAD is supported by both commands in the conduct of missions assigned to NORAD. NORAD provides bi-national situation awareness of the aerospace and maritime domains to CJOC and USNORTHCOM.

**6. North American Aerospace Defense Command Subordinate Commands**

a. NORAD aerospace warning and air control operations are conducted by its three subordinate regions. Each region has an air operations center and is further subdivided into one or more ADSs for tactical execution. The ADS operates a battle control center (BCC), a tactical C2 node that supports air battle management, air weapons control, surveillance and identification, data links and airspace management.

b. Each BCC contains a combat mission crew and battle staff. When formed, the battle staff directs sector air control activities. The BCC operates on a continuous basis and closely coordinates air sovereignty activities with FAA air traffic control centers to ensure HD activities can be safely and successfully executed.

c. NORAD tactical level operations also include ground based air defense units in fixed locations such as the NCR and temporary sites, as needed, to support national special security events. Units supporting temporary sites (e.g., USAF control and reporting centers and airborne warning and control systems) share air picture information with the associated BCC. A more detailed description of each of the three NORAD regions is provided below.

(1) **Alaskan NORAD Region.** ANR is the bi-national organization responsible for performing the NORAD air sovereignty and air control mission over the state of Alaska as well as the northwest approaches to North America. HQ ANR is collocated at Joint Base Elmendorf-Richardson, Alaska, with HQ US ALCOM, a subunified command of USPACOM and JTF-AK, a standing C2 HQ of USNORTHCOM. The ANR Commander is also the Commander, 11th Air Force, as well as commander of ALCOM and JTF-AK. ANR is supported by both active duty Canadian forces and US forces, as well as Alaska ANG units. The ANR's BCC is manned by both US personnel and Canadian forces to maintain continuous surveillance of its OA. The Alaska Air Defense Sector is the single ADS within the ANR and is collocated at Joint Base Elmendorf-Richardson.

(2) **Canadian North American Aerospace Defense Command Region (CANR).** CANR is the bi-national organization responsible for performing NORAD's air sovereignty and air control mission over Canada as well as the polar approaches to North America. CANR is located at Canadian Forces Base (CFB) Winnipeg, Manitoba. The BCC for Canada is located at CFB North Bay, Ontario. The CANR Commander is also the Commander of 1 CAD. CANR is manned by both 1 CAD and US personnel.

(3) **Continental United States NORAD Region.** CONR is the subordinate, bi-nationally staffed command responsible for the air sovereignty and air control of the airspace over the CONUS, to include the approaches to North America. The CONR Commander exercises OPCON over all air defense forces within CONUS. CONR operates in an extremely complex, bi-national and multi-command environment where political, military, and economic conditions interrelate. CONR is collocated with a numbered air force subordinate to Air Combat Command. The CONR Commander is also the CDR

AFNORTH, and may be designated the JFACC for USNORTHCOM for unilateral US air operations within the USNORTHCOM AOR. CONR ADSs and the NCR-IADS are identified below.

(a) **NCR-IADS.** NCR-IADS consists of two tactical C2 entities that provide air defense for the NCR under the OPCON of the CONR commander. The Eastern Air Defense Sector (EADS) is responsible for surveillance, identification and air intercept operations while the Joint Air Defense Operations Center (JADOC) provides ground based air defense forces to complement EADS capabilities. EADS and JADOC coordinate on all air tracks of interest within the NCR.

(b) **Eastern Air Defense Sector.** EADS, located at Rome Air National Guard Base, New York. EADS is responsible for all CONR air operations east of the western boundary of the following states: Wisconsin, Illinois, Kentucky, Tennessee, and Alabama.

(c) **Western Air Defense Sector (WADS).** WADS, located at Joint Base Lewis-McChord, Washington, is responsible for all CONR air operations west of the eastern boundary of the following states: Minnesota, Iowa, Missouri, Arkansas, and Mississippi.

## 7. Other Forces

a. **US Element NORAD.** USELEMNORAD is an organizational construct created in response to the requirements of Title 10, USC, which specifies that US military forces must be kept in a US military "chain-of-command," and may not be assigned directly to a multinational or bi-national command. CDRUSELEMNORAD is the senior US officer assigned to NORAD.

b. **First Canadian Air Division.** Winnipeg, Manitoba is home to the dual HQ for 1 CAD and the CANR. The headquarters serves as the central point of C2 for Canada's operational Air Force and oversees the monitoring of Canada's airspace in support of commitments to NORAD.

# APPENDIX D
## KEY HOMELAND DEFENSE LEGAL AND POLICY DOCUMENTS

### 1. Legal Framework, National Policy, and Strategic Guidance

Multiple documents provide guidance for the HD mission.

a. **The Constitution.** The Preamble states that two of the purposes of the Constitution are to ensure domestic tranquility and provide for the common defense. Furthermore, Congress has the power to declare war, raise and support armies, provide and maintain a Navy, and provide for calling forth the militia to execute the laws of the Union, suppress insurrections, and repel invasions. The President is the Commander in Chief of the Armed Forces. In Article 4, the Constitution provides the basis for HD by requiring the US to protect each state against invasion.

b. **Key Executive and Legislative Guidance.** The following documents are key references when HD operations are addressed:

(1) Title 10, USC, *Armed Forces.* Title 10, USC, provides guidance on the Armed Forces of the US. Guidance is divided into the following subtitles: one on general military law and one each for the US Army, the US Navy and US Marine Corps, the US Air Force and Air Force Auxiliary (Civil Air Patrol), and the RC.

(2) Titles 14, 33, 46, and 50, USC. These statutes define the statutory authority for the USCG to conduct HD and HS missions.

(3) Title 32, USC, establishes the basis for federal oversight of the NG, and provides the authority for the NG to conduct activities in a federal duty status, subject to state control. The majority of activities conducted pursuant to Title 32, USC, directly relate to training or other readiness requirements established by the Army and the Air Force in order to prepare the NG for its warfighting mission. NG forces will be employed in HD missions when mobilized into a Title 10 status. The only exception to this is under Title 32, USC, Section 902, which authorizes SecDef to provide funds to state governors for NG forces to perform specified HD "activities" without first activating these forces under Title 10, USC, status.

(4) Title 50, USC, *War and National Defense.* Title 50, USC, contains federal law pertaining to war and national defense. Among the major provisions of Title 50, USC, are: authorizing the detention and removal of foreign nationals from the US; authorizing financial reward for information on nuclear material/weapons; and regulating vessel anchorage and movement during a national emergency.

(5) Presidential Policy Directive (PPD)-1, *Organization of the National Security Council System.* PPD-1 describes the organization of the NSC as the principal forum for consideration of national security policy issues requiring Presidential determination. The

NSC, along with its associated committees, advises and assists integration of all aspects of national security policy as it affects the US. The NSC IPCs are the main day-to-day fora for interagency coordination of national security policy.

(6) PPD-8, *National Preparedness.* This directive is aimed at strengthening the security and resilience of the US through systematic preparation for the threats that pose the greatest risk to the Nation, including acts of terrorism, cyberspace attacks, pandemics, and catastrophic national disasters.

(7) PPD-10, *US Ballistic Missile Defenses* (replaces NSPD 23, *National Policy on Ballistic Missile Defense).* PPD-10 acknowledges that ballistic missile systems present an increasingly important challenge and threat to the security of the US, its deployed forces, and its allies and partners. PPD-10 provides policy and guidelines for the development and deployment of US BMDs.

(8) HSPD-4/NSPD-17, *National Strategy to Combat Weapons of Mass Destruction.* HSPD-4 states that nuclear, biological, and chemical weapons in the possession of hostile states and terrorists represent one of the greatest security challenges facing the United States and that we must pursue a comprehensive strategy to counter this threat. The strategy describes three pillars: counterproliferation to combat WMD use; strengthen nonproliferation to combat WMD proliferation; and WMD consequence management in response to WMD use. Each pillar lists specific actions to be pursued within its purview.

(9) HSPD-7, *Critical Infrastructure Identification, Prioritization, and Protection.* HSPD-7 establishes a national policy for federal departments and agencies to identify and prioritize US CI/KR and to protect them from terrorist attacks. This directive identifies roles and responsibilities of the Secretary of HS and other departments and agencies and recognizes DOD as the sector-specific agency for the DIB.

(10) HSPD-10/NSPD-33, *Biodefense for the 21st Century.* HSPD-10 provides a comprehensive framework for US biodefense and, among other things, delineates the roles and responsibilities of federal agencies and departments in continuing their work in this area.

(11) HSPD-11, *Comprehensive Terrorist-Related Screening Procedures.* HSPD-11 establishes procedures to enhance terrorist-related screening through comprehensive, coordinated procedures that detect, identify, track, and interdict people, cargo, conveyances, and other entities and objects that pose a threat to HS.

(12) HSPD-12, *Policy for a Common Identification Standard for Federal Employees and Contractors.* HSPD-12 establishes a policy of the US to enhance security, increase government efficiency, reduce identity fraud, and protect personal privacy by establishing a mandatory, government-wide standard for secure and reliable forms of identification issued by the federal government to its employees and contractors.

(13) HSPD-13/NSPD-41, *Maritime Security Policy.* HSPD-13 establishes US policy, guidelines, and implementation actions to enhance US national security and HS by protecting US maritime interests.

(14) HSPD-14/NSPD-43, *Domestic Nuclear Detection Office.* HSPD-14 establishes the DNDO within DHS and assigns it the responsibility to develop the global nuclear detection architecture and to acquire and support the deployment of the domestic detection system. It directs DOD to conduct close cooperation and coordination with DNDO.

(15) HSPD-16/NSPD-47, *Aviation Security Policy.* This directive establishes US policy, guidelines, and implementation actions to continue the enhancement of HS and national security by protecting the US and its interests from threats in the air domain. It directs multiple USG departments (including DOD) and agencies to accomplish specific tasks that will improve the security and defense of the US homeland. Specifically, it directs protection of critical transportation networks and infrastructure, enhancement of situational awareness, and enhancement of international relationships with allies and other partners.

(16) HSPD-18, *Medical Countermeasures Against Weapons of Mass Destruction.* This HSPD establishes policy guidelines to draw upon the public and private sector scientific communities to address medical countermeasure requirements relating to CBRN threats. However, SecDef retains exclusive responsibility for research, development, acquisition, and deployment of medical countermeasures to prevent or mitigate the health effects of WMD threats and naturally occurring threats to the Armed Forces and continues to direct strategic planning for and oversight of programs to support medical countermeasures development and acquisition for Armed Forces personnel.

(17) HSPD-19, *Combating Terrorist Use of Explosives in the United States.* This directive establishes a national policy, and calls for the development of a national strategy and implementation plan on the prevention and detection of, protection against, and response to terrorist use of explosives in the US. DOD participates in the maintenance of secure information-sharing systems that make information available, through DHS control, to LEAs for use in enhancing US preparedness to prevent, detect, protect against, and respond to such attacks.

(18) HSPD-20/NSPD-51, *National Continuity Policy.* This directive establishes a comprehensive national policy on the continuity of federal government structures and operations. It emphasizes the importance of a comprehensive national program and provides continuity guidance and requirements involving all government levels and the private sector for integrated and scalable continuity planning. It directs DOD, in coordination with DHS, to provide secure, integrated, COG communications to the President, the Vice President, and, at a minimum, Category I executive departments and agencies.

(19) Presidential Decision Directive (PDD)-24, *US Counterintelligence Effectiveness.* PDD-24 fosters increased cooperation, coordination and accountability among all US CI agencies. It directs the creation of a new national CI policy structure under the auspices of the NSC and directs the creation of a new National CI Center. Nothing in this directive amends or changes the authorities and responsibilities of SecDef.

(20) EO 12333, *United States Intelligence Activities,* as Amended. This EO provides for the national security of the US through the production of timely, accurate, and

insightful information about the activities, capabilities, plans, and intentions of foreign powers, organizations, and persons, and their agents. Special emphasis is placed on threats due to espionage, terrorism, and the development, possession, proliferation, or use of WMD. It both recognizes the critical partnerships with state, local, tribal, and private sector entities that support this EO's goals and also the obligation to fully protect the legal rights, freedoms, civil liberties, and privacy rights of US persons guaranteed under federal law in achieving these goals.

(21) EO 13223, *Ordering the Ready Reserves of Armed Forces to Active Duty and Delegating Certain Authorities to the Secretary of Defense and the Secretary of Transportation.* This EO resulted from the 14 September 2001 Presidential Proclamation 7463: Declaration of National Emergency by Reason of Certain Terrorist Attacks and recognition of immediate threat of further attacks on the US. It provides the DOD and DOT (now DHS) additional authorities, among them the ability to order any unit or member of the Ready Reserve to active duty and the transfer of select Title 10, USC, provisions from the President to the respective department secretaries.

(22) EO 13231, *Critical Infrastructure Protection in the Information Age* (as amended). This EO is designed to ensure the protection of information systems for critical infrastructure, including EP communications, and the physical assets that support such systems. It establishes national policy, scope of effort, and expands the National Infrastructure Advisory Council. The order specifically assigns SecDef and Director of Central Intelligence with responsibility for their respective National Security Information Systems.

(23) *Military Order of 13 November 2001, Federal Register: (Volume 66, Number 57833).* This military order from the President declared a state of armed conflict exists since various terrorist attacks against the US, and requires the use of the armed forces of the US. It acknowledges the use of the armed forces to identify terrorists and their supporters, to disrupt their activities, and to eliminate their ability to conduct or support terrorist attacks.

(24) EO 13292, *Further Amendment to Executive Order 12958,* as Amended, Classified National Security Information. This EO prescribes a uniform system for classifying, safeguarding, and declassifying national security information, including information relating to defense against transnational terrorism.

(25) EO 13354, *National Counterterrorism Center.* This EO established the NCTC under the auspices of the Director of Central Intelligence. The center is intended to strengthen intelligence analysis and strategic planning and intelligence support to operations to counter transnational terrorist threats against the territory, people, and interests of the US. Support is intended for all agencies (includes DOD) consistent with applicable law.

(26) EO 13381, Strengthening Processes Relating to Determining Eligibility for Access to Classified National Security Information. EO 13381 addresses the protection of classified national security information against unauthorized disclosure and agency functions relating to determining eligibility for access to classified national security information.

(27) EO 13388, *Further Strengthening the Sharing of Terrorism Information to Protect America*. This further strengthens the effective conduct of US CT activities and is intended to protect the territory, people and interests of the US, including against terrorist attacks.

(28) EO 13581, *Blocking Property of Transnational Criminal Organizations*. Determines that significant TCOs constitute an unusual and extraordinary threat to the national security, foreign policy, and economy of the US, and declares a national emergency to deal with that threat.

(29) *The National Strategy for Homeland Security (2007)*. This document lays out the strategic objectives, organization, and critical areas for HS. The strategy identifies critical areas that focus on preventing terrorist attacks, reducing the nation's vulnerabilities, minimizing the damage and recovering from attacks that do occur. These critical areas are compatible with DOD's framework for HS that is discussed in this publication.

(30) *National Security Strategy (NSS), the National Defense Strategy, and NMS*. The *NSS*, signed by the President, establishes broad strategic guidance for advancing US interests in the global environment through the instruments of national power. The *National Defense Strategy (NDS)* is a distillation of the *NSS*, gives strategic guidance specific to the DOD and is signed by the SecDef. The *NMS*, signed by the CJCS and derived from the *NSS*, focuses on how the armed forces of the US will be employed to accomplish national strategic objectives. The *NSS* and the NMS continue to reflect the first and fundamental commitment to defend the US against its adversaries.

(31) *National Strategy for the Physical Protection of Critical Infrastructures and Key Assets*. This document defines the road ahead for a core mission area identified in the *National Strategy for HS*, reducing the nation's vulnerability to acts of terrorism by protecting US critical infrastructures and key assets from physical attack. It identifies a clear set of national goals and objectives to achieve protection goals. The strategy identifies thirteen critical infrastructure sectors. Key asset protection represents a broad array of unique facilities, sites, and structures whose disruption or destruction could have significant consequences across multiple dimensions

(32) *National Strategy to Secure Cyberspace*. This strategy outlines an initial framework for both organizing and prioritizing efforts to secure cyberspace. It provides direction to the USG departments and agencies that have roles in cyberspace security and identifies steps, that state, local, and tribal governments, private companies and organizations, and individual Americans can do to improve collective cybersecurity. The strategy identifies three strategic objectives: prevent attacks in cyberspace against American critical infrastructure; reduce national vulnerability to attacks in cyberspace; and minimize damage and recovery time from attacks in cyberspace that do occur.

(33) *National Infrastructure Protection Plan*. The *National Infrastructure Protection Plan* provides a unifying framework that integrates a range of efforts designed to enhance the safety of the nation's critical infrastructure. The overarching goal of the *National Infrastructure Protection Plan* is to build a safer, more secure, and more resilient

America by preventing, deterring, neutralizing, or mitigating the effects of a terrorist attack or natural disaster, and to strengthen national preparedness, response, and recovery in the event of an emergency.

(34) *National Strategy for Maritime Security.* This document aligns all federal government maritime security programs and initiatives into a comprehensive and cohesive national effort involving appropriate federal, state, local, and private sector entities. There are eight supporting plans which, when combined with the national strategy, present a comprehensive national effort to promote global economic stability and protect legitimate activities while preventing hostile or illegal acts within the maritime domain. The document provides three broad principles as overarching guidance for maritime security that: outline a vision for a fully coordinated USG effort to protect US interests in the maritime domain; provide an overarching plan addressing all of the components of the maritime domain including domestic, international, public, and private components; and incorporate a global, cross-disciplined approach centered on a layered, defense-in-depth framework, adjusted per the threat level.

(35) *National Southwest Border Counter Narcotics Strategy.* This document addresses the land and air domains of the southwest border and the Mexican approaches and includes tasks for DOD. The Strategy affirms that the USG's CD, CT, and immigration enforcement missions are interrelated and serves as an integrated component of the nation's efforts to secure the southwest border against all threats to the health and safety of the American people.

(36) *Strategy to Combat Transnational Organized Crime.* This strategy applies all instruments of national power to protect citizens and US national security interests from the convergence of 21st century transnational criminal threats. The strategy is organized around a single unifying principle to build, balance, and integrate the tools of American power to combat transnational organized crime and related threats to national security and urge our foreign partners to do the same.

(37) *National Strategy for Aviation Security.* The strategy presents a vision for aviation security aimed at securing the people and interests of the US. It underscores the Nation's commitment to strengthening international partnerships and advancing economic well-being around the globe by facilitating commerce and abiding by the principles of freedom of the airways.

(38) *National Strategy for Countering Biological Threats.* The strategy presents a framework for future USG planning efforts that supports HSPD-10/NSPD-33, Bio-defense for the 21st Century and complements existing Presidential strategies related to biological threat preparedness and response.

(39) *National Strategy for Counterterrorism.* This strategy articulates the USG approach to countering terrorism and identifies the range of tools critical to the strategy's success. Regarding the homeland, it cites the continuing need for robust defensive efforts to prevent terrorists from entering the US or from operating freely inside US borders. It identifies the capabilities and resources of state, local, and tribal entities to serve as a

powerful force multiplier for the USG's CT efforts, and also emphasizes vigilance against both overseas-based threats and against US based terrorist activity, whether the terrorists are focused domestically or on plotting to attack overseas targets.

(40) The Canada-United States Basic Defense Document (CANUS BDD). This document requires the Commanders of NORAD, USNORTHCOM, and CJOC to establish closer relationships with each other and with supporting agencies to ensure a timely and coordinated response to defense and security challenges to Canada and the US.

(41) North American Aerospace Defense Agreement. This is an agreement between the Government of the US of America and the Government of Canada on NORAD. It establishes the primary missions of NORAD: aerospace warning, aerospace control, and maritime warning.

(42) *Canada—US Civil Assistance Plan (CANUS Civil Assistance Plan) (2012)*. The *CANUS Civil Assistance Plan* provides a framework for the military forces of one nation to support the military forces of the other nation while providing military support of civil authorities. Guidance in the 2006 Canada-US Basic Defense Document directs Commander, USNORTHCOM to "develop detailed plans for the defense and security of Canada and the US." The *CANUS Civil Assistance Plan* was originally developed and signed in February 2008. Subsequently, CJOC and USNORTHCOM worked together to provide support for both a short-notice event and pre-planning for a major event. An updated version of the plan was signed in 2012.

(43) *Canada—US Combined Defense Plan (CANUS CDP) (2012)*. The *CANUS CDP* provides a framework for the combined defense of Canada and the US during peace, contingencies, and war, as tasked by the CANUS BDD. The *CANUS CDP* is a framework plan to address: coordinated/combined military operations in/across multiple domains, as directed by national authorities and in conjunction with other plans; outline legal authorities and protocols; provide C2 options; and reinforce Tri-Command collaboration and information sharing. The designated planning agents for the *CANUS CDP* are USNORTHCOM and CJOC. Operations under the *CANUS CDP* could occur in multiple domains and may be executed when there is a common perceived threat or one or both nations are under attack.

(44) Memorandum of Understanding Between the Intelligence Community, Federal LEAs, and the DHS Security Concerning Information Sharing. This agreement provides the framework and guidance to govern information sharing, use, and handling among the following individuals and their agencies: Secretary of Homeland Security; Director of Central Intelligence; the Attorney General; and any other organization having federal LE responsibilities (other than those that are part of the DHS). The agreement mandates minimum requirements for information sharing, use, and handling and for coordination and deconfliction of analytic judgments.

**2. Department of Defense Policy and Guidance**

a. **Implications.** Specific authorities for HD missions are contained in federal and state law and policy documents. These form the basis for the development of DOD guidelines. These guidelines are promulgated in a variety of methods that include national strategy documents, planning guidance, and DODDs. These policy documents are consistent with and complementary to the federal statutes and guidelines discussed earlier in this appendix. DODDs specifically address missions.

b. **Key DOD Guidance.** The following discussion identifies some of the key documents that may assist commanders and staffs in the planning and execution of the HD mission areas.

(1) *Joint Strategy Review (JSR).* The JSR helps the Joint Staff integrate strategy, operational planning, and program assessments. It covers the short, mid and long-term periods: 0-2, 2-10, and 10-20 years in the future. The JSR assesses the global strategic setting for issues affecting the NMS.

(2) *Unified Command Plan.* The UCP, developed by DOD and approved by the President, provides basic guidance to all unified CCDRs, establishes their missions, responsibilities, the general geographical AORs for geographic CCDRs, and specifies functional responsibilities for functional CCDRs.

(3) *Defense Planning Guidance (DPG).* This document, issued by SecDef, provides firm guidance in the form of goals, priorities, and objectives, including fiscal constraints, for the development of the program objective memorandums by the Military Departments and DOD agencies.

(4) *Guidance for Employment of the Force.* The GEF translates national security objectives and high-level strategy found in the NSS and other strategic reviews, into DOD priorities and comprehensive planning direction to guide the DOD services and agencies in the employment of DOD forces. The GEF conveys guidance approved by the President for contingency planning, as well as SecDef's regional, functional, DOD security cooperation priorities and planning guidance, and general planning guidance. In addition to guiding internal DOD planning efforts, it also directs that DOD plans are, to the appropriate extent, informed by, coordinated with, and synchronized with the activities of relevant non-DOD organizations, which is especially important for several HD missions with regard to planning and conducting operations. The GEF guides resource constrained planning so as to balance both near-term and long-term strategic risks.

(5) *Strategic Military Intelligence Review (SIR).* The SIR establishes core intelligence issues of highest priority, identifies needs and gaps, and provides a common framework and substantive guidance for allocating intelligence collection and production resources.

(6) DODI 2000.12, *DOD Antiterrorism (AT) Program.* This directive updates policies and assigns responsibilities for implementing the procedures for DOD's AT program. It establishes the CJCS as the principal advisor and focal point responsible to

SecDef for DOD AT issues. It also defines the AT responsibilities of the Military Departments, CCMDs, DOD agencies, and DOD field activities. Its guidelines are applicable for the physical security of all DOD activities, both overseas and in the homeland.

(7) DODD-S-2060.04, *DOD Support to the National Technical Nuclear Forensics Program.* This directive describes policies and assigns responsibilities for DOD support to the National Technical Nuclear Forensics Program. DOD supports the national effort to attribute nuclear threats to their source, which helps deter aggressors from considering the use of nuclear weapons, as well as deterring follow-on attacks through collection and analysis of post-detonation samples and data. DOD must be prepared to deploy air and ground sample collection assets and to conduct post-detonation laboratory analysis, evaluation, and reporting activities.

(8) DODD 3020.40, *DOD Policy and Responsibilities for Critical Infrastructure.* This document establishes policy and assigns responsibilities for DCI activities as they apply to DOD. It also authorizes ASD (HD&ASA) to issue instructions and guidance for the implementation of this directive. Its companion instruction, DODI 3020.45, Defense Critical Infrastructure Program (DCIP) Management, implements management of the identification, prioritization, and assessment of DCI as a comprehensive program. The program that includes the development of adaptive plans and procedures to mitigate risk; the restoration of capability in the event of loss or degradation; incident management; and protection of DCI-related sensitive information.

(9) DODD 3160.01, *Homeland Defense Activities Conducted by the National Guard.* This directive establishes DOD policy and assigns responsibilities for employing the NG to conduct HD activities IAW Title 32, USC. SecDef may provide funds for governors to employ the NG in their control to conduct HD activities that SecDef determines to be necessary and appropriate and funds that the individual governors may request for deliberately planned activities or due to exceptional circumstances.

(10) DODD 5105.77, *National Guard Bureau,* establishes policy for and defines the organization and management, responsibilities and functions, relationships, and authorities of the Chief, NGB, and establishes the NGB as a joint activity of DOD.

(11) DODD 5111.13, *Assistant Secretary of Defense for Homeland Defense and Americas Security Affairs.* Under the authority, direction, and control of USD(P), serves as the principal civilian advisor to SecDef and the USD(P) on HD activities, DSCA, and Western Hemisphere security matters.

(12) DODD 5200.27, *Acquisition of Information Concerning Persons and Organizations not Affiliated with DOD.* This document establishes the Defense Investigative Program general policy, limitations, procedures, and operational guidance pertaining to the collecting, processing, storing, and disseminating of information concerning persons and organizations not affiliated with DOD.

(13) DODD 5205.02, *DOD Operations Security Program.* This document provides policy and responsibilities which govern DOD's OPSEC program and incorporates the

requirements of National Security Decision Directive 298 that apply to DOD. It underscores the importance of OPSEC and how it is integrated into military operations on a daily basis.

(14) DODD 5240.01, *DOD Intelligence Activities.* This provides guidance to DOD intelligence components to collect, retain, or disseminate information concerning US persons. Another companion publication, DOD 5240.1-R, Procedures Governing the Activities of DOD Intelligence Components that Affect United States Persons, itemizes DOD intelligence components' sole authority by which such components may: collect, retain and disseminate information concerning US persons; employment of certain collection techniques to obtain information for foreign intelligence and CI purposes; and implementation of those policies that govern other aspects of DOD intelligence activities, including the oversight of such activities.

(15) CJCSI 3100.01B, *Joint Strategic Planning System.* This document provides joint policy and guidance on, and describes the responsibilities and functions of, the joint strategic planning system. It provides expanded guidance on the process for developing CCMD theater engagement plans and identifies the plan approval process.

(16) CJCSI 3110.01H, *Joint Strategic Capabilities Plan.* The JSCP provides guidance to CCDRs, Service Chiefs, Joint Staff, CSA directors, applicable defense agency and directors of DOD field activities, and the NGB, to accomplish tasks and missions based on near-term military capabilities. The JSCP implements campaign, contingency, and posture planning guidance reflected in the GEF.

(17) CJCSI 3121.01B, *Standing Rules of Engagement /Standing Rules for the Use of Force for US Forces (U).* This instruction establishes rules regarding the use of force by DOD personnel during military operations.

(18) CJCSI 3213.01, *Joint Operations Security.* This provides policy and guidance for planning and executing OPSEC in support of joint military operations.

(19) CJCSI 3610.01C, *Aircraft Piracy (Hijacking) and Destruction of Derelict Airborne Objects.* This CJCSI provides guidance to the Deputy Director for Operations, National Military Command Center, and operational commanders in the event of an aircraft piracy (hijacking) or request for destruction of derelict airborne objects.

(20) CJCSI 5221.01, *Delegation of Authority to Commanders of Combatant Commands to Disclose Classified Military Information to Foreign Governments and International Organizations.* This instruction explains the authority delegated by CJCS to the CCDRs concerning the disclosure of classified military information for which they are the originating component to foreign governments and international organizations.

(21) CJCSI 5810.01, *Implementation of the DOD Law of War Program.* This document establishes joint policy, assigns responsibilities, and provides guidance regarding the US law of war obligations. It also assigns specific responsibilities within DOD to ensure compliance with the law of war.

(22) Memorandum of Agreement Between the Department of Defense and Department of Homeland Security for Department of Defense Support to the US Coast Guard for Maritime Homeland Security. This memorandum identifies and documents appropriate capabilities, roles, missions, and functions for DOD in support of the USCG when conducting maritime HS operations, and to facilitate the rapid flow of DOD forces to the USCG in support of such operations.

(23) Memorandum of Agreement between Department of Defense and Department of Homeland Security for the Inclusion of the US Coast Guard in support of Maritime Homeland Defense. This establishes a DOD joint C2 structure for maritime HD operations that include USCG forces and identifies and documents appropriate roles, missions, and functions for the USCG in support of maritime HD operations.

Intentionally Blank

# APPENDIX E
## REFERENCES

The development of JP 3-27 is based on the following primary references:

**1. General**

    a.  US Constitution.

    b.  Canada-United States (CANUS) Rush-Bagot Treaty.

    c.  CANUS Basic Defense Document.

    d.  Executive Order (EO) 12333, *United States Intelligence Activities.*

    e.  EO 12656, *Assignment of Emergency Preparedness Responsibilities.*

    f. EO 13223, *Ordering the Ready Reserves of Armed Forces to Active Duty and Delegating Certain Authorities to the Secretary of Defense and the Secretary of Transportation.*

    g.  EO 13228, *Establishing the Office of Homeland Security and the Homeland Security Council.*

    h.  EO 13231, *Critical Infrastructure Protection in the Information Age.*

    i.  EO 13354, *National Counterterrorism Center.*

    j.  EO 13381, *Strengthening Processes Relating to Determining Eligibility for Access to Classified National Security Information.*

    k.  EO 13385, *Continuance of Certain Federal Advisory Committees.*

    l. EO 13388, *Further Strengthening the Sharing of Terrorism Information to Protect Americans.*

    m.  HSPD-1, *Organization and Operations of the Homeland Security Council.*

    n.  HSPD-2, *Combating Terrorism Through Immigration Policies.*

    o.  HSPD-4/NSPD-17, *National Strategy to Combat Weapons of Mass Destruction.*

    p.  HSPD-5, *Management of Domestic Incidents.*

    q.  HSPD-6, *Integration and Use of Screening Information.*

    r.  HSPD-7, *Critical Infrastructure Identification, Prioritization, and Protection.*

    s.  HSPD-10/NSPD-33, *Bio-defense for the 21st Century.*

t.  HSPD-11, *Comprehensive Terrorist-Related Screening Procedures.*

u.  HSPD-12, *Policy for a Common Identification Standard for Federal Employees and Contractors.*

v.  HSPD-13/NSPD-41, *Maritime Security Policy.*

w.  HSPD-14/NSPD-43, *Domestic Nuclear Detection Office.*

x.  HSPD-15/NSPD-46, *US Policy and Strategy in the War on Terror[ism].*

y.  HSPD-16/NSPD-47, *US Aviation Security Policy.*

zz.  HSPD-18, *Medical Countermeasures Against Weapons of Mass Destruction.*

aa.  HSPD-19, *Combating Terrorist Use of Explosives in the United States.*

bb.  HSPD-20, *National Continuity Policy.*

cc.  HSPD-23, *Cyber Security and Monitoring.*

dd.  *Maritime Operational Threat Response Plan.*

ee.  Maritime Strategy for Homeland Security.

ff.  Military Order of 13 November 2001.

gg.  National Industrial Security Program.

hh.  *National Intelligence Strategy of the United States of America.*

ii.  *National Defense Strategy.*

jj.  *National Military Strategy.*

kk.  *National Security Strategy.*

ll.  *National Response Framework.*

mm.  *National Strategy for Combating Terrorism.*

nn.  *Strategy to Combat Transnational Organized Crime.*

oo.  *National Strategy for Homeland Security.*

pp.  *National Strategy for Physical Protection of Critical Infrastructure and Key Assets.*

qq.  *National Strategy to Secure Cyberspace.*

rr.  *National Strategy for Maritime Security.*

ss. The North American Aerospace Defense Command (NORAD) Agreement and Terms of Reference.

tt. Operation NOBLE EAGLE (ONE) Tactics, Techniques and Procedures Reference Guide.

uu. PPD-1, *Organization of the National Security Council System.*

vv. PPD-8, *National Preparedness.*

ww. PPD-10, *US Ballistic Missile Defenses.*

xx. PDD-14, *Counternarcotics.*

yy. PDD-24, *US Counterintelligence.*

zz. PDD-67, *Enduring Constitutional Government and Continuity of Government Operations.*

aaa. Title 10, USC, *Armed Forces.*

bbb. Title 14, USC, *United States Coast Guard.*

ccc. Title 18, USC, Section 1385, The Posse Comitatus Act.

ddd. Title 32, USC, *National Guard.*

eee. Title 33, USC, *Navigation and Navigable Waters.*

fff. Title 46, USC, *Shipping.*

ggg. Title 50, USC, *War and National Defense.*

hhh. Uniting and Strengthening America by Providing Appropriate Tools Required to Intercept and Obstruct Terrorism Act (USA PATRIOT Act as amended).

## 2. Department of Defense Documents

a. Ballistic Missile Defense Review Report.

b. Contingency Planning Guidance.

c. DODD 3020.26, *Defense Continuity Program.*

d. DODD 3020.36, *Assignment of National Security EP(NSEP) Responsibilities to DOD Components.*

e. DODD 3020.40, *DOD Policies and Responsibilities for Critical Infrastructure Protection.*

f. DODD 3160.01, *Homeland Defense Activities Conducted by the National Guard.*

g. DODD 5100.01, *Functions of the DOD and Its Major Components.*

h. DODD 5100.78, *United States Port Security Program.*

i. DODD 5105.19, *Defense Information Systems Agency (DISA).*

j. DODD 5105.21, *Defense Intelligence Agency.*

k. DODD 5105.77, *National Guard Bureau (NGB).*

l. DODD 5105.83, *National Guard Joint Force Headquarters-State (NG JFHQ-State).*

m. DODD 5148.11, *Assistant to the Secretary of Defense for Intelligence Oversight (ATSD IO).*

n. DODD 5200.27, *Acquisition of Information Concerning Persons and Organizations not Affiliated with the DOD.*

o. DODD 5205.02, *DOD Operations Security (OPSEC) Program.*

p. DODD 5210.56, *Carrying of Firearms and the Use of Force by DOD Personnel Engaged in Security, Law and Order, or Counterintelligence Activities.*

q. DODI 5220.22, *National Industrial Security Program.*

r. DODD 5240.01, *DOD Intelligence Activities.*

s. DOD 5240.1-R, *Procedures Governing the Activities of DOD Intelligence Components that Affect United States Persons.*

t. DODD 5525.5, *DOD Cooperation with Civilian Law Enforcement Officials.*

u. DODD 8001.01, *Global Information Grid.*

v. DODD 8500.01E, *Information Assurance.*

w. DODI 2000.12, *DOD Antiterrorism (AT) Program.*

x. DODI 2000.16, *DOD Antiterrorism Standards.*

y. DODI 3000.05, *Stability Operations.*

z. DODI 3020.45, *Defense Critical Infrastructure Program (DCIP) Management.*

aa. DODI 3020.52, *DOD Installation Chemical, Biological, Radiological, Nuclear, and High-Yield Explosive (CBRNE) Preparedness Standards.*

bb. DODI 3025.21, *Defense Support of Civilian Law Enforcement Agencies.*

cc. DODI 5220.22, *National Industrial Security Program.*

dd. DODI 6055.17, *DOD Installation Emergency Management (IEM) Program.*

ee. UFC 4-010-01, *DOD Minimum Standards for Buildings.*

ff. DOD Manual 3020.45, Volume I, *Defense Critical Infrastructure Program (DCIP): DOD Mission-Based Critical Asset Identification Process (CAIP).*

gg. Global Force Management Guidance. Section II, *Assignment of Forces (Forces For Unified Commands).*

hh. Joint Planning Guidance.

ii. *Joint Strategic Capabilities Plan.*

jj. Memorandum of Agreement Between the Department of Defense and the Department of Homeland Security for Inclusion of the US Coast Guard in Support of Maritime Homeland Defense.

kk. Memorandum of Agreement Between the Department of Defense and the Department of Homeland Security for Department of Defense Support to the United States Coast Guard for Maritime Homeland Security.

ll. National Defense Strategy of the United States of America.

mm. National Geospatial Intelligence Agency Geospatial Intelligence Series (GIPS).

nn. National Military Strategy for Cyberspace Operations.

oo. Strategic Planning Guidance.

pp. Strategy for Homeland Defense and Civil Support.

qq. *Unified Command Plan.*

3. **Chairman of the Joint Chiefs of Staff Issuances**

    a. JP 1, *Doctrine for the Armed Forces of the United States.*

    b. JP 1-0, *Joint Personnel Support.*

    c. JP 1-05, *Religious Affairs in Joint Operations.*

    d. JP 2-0, *Joint Intelligence.*

    e. JP 2-01, *Joint and National Intelligence Support to Military Operations.*

f. JP 3-0, *Joint Operations.*

g. JP 3-01, *Countering Air and Missile Threats.*

h. JP 3-03, *Joint Interdiction.*

i. JP 3-07.2, *Antiterrorism.*

j. JP 3-07.4, *Counterdrug Operations.*

k. JP 3-08, *Interorganizational Coordination During Joint Operations.*

l. JP 3-09.3, *Close Air Support (CAS).*

m. JP 3-11, *Operations in Chemical, Biological, Radiological and Nuclear (CBRN) Environments.*

n. JP 3-12, *Cyberspace Operations.*

o. JP 3-13, *Information Operations.*

p. JP 3-13.2, *Military Information Support Operations.*

q. JP 3-13.3, *Operations Security.*

r. JP 3-14, *Space Operations.*

s. JP 3-16, *Multinational Operations.*

t. JP 3-28, *Defense Support of Civil Authorities.*

u. JP 3-30, *Command and Control for Joint Air Operations.*

v. JP 3-31, *Command and Control for Joint Land Operations.*

w. JP 3-32, *Command and Control for Joint Maritime Operations.*

x. JP 3-33, *Joint Task Force Headquarters.*

y. JP 3-34, *Joint Engineer Operations.*

z. JP 3-35, *Deployment and Redeployment Operations.*

aa. JP 3-40, *Countering Weapons of Mass Destruction.*

bb. JP 3-41, *Chemical, Biological, Radiological, and Nuclear Consequence Management.*

cc. JP 3-52, *Joint Airspace Control.*

dd. JP 3-60, *Joint Targeting.*

ee. JP 3-61, *Public Affairs.*

ff. JP 4-0, *Joint Logistics.*

gg. JP 4-02, *Health Services.*

hh. JP 4-05, *Joint Mobilization Planning.*

ii. JP4-06, *Mortuary Affairs.*

jj. JP 5-0, *Joint Operation Planning.*

kk. JP 6-0, *Joint Communications System.*

ll. CJCSI 1301.01D, *Joint Individual Augmentation Procedures.*

mm. CJCSI 3100.01B, *Joint Strategic Planning System.*

nn. CJCSI 3121.01B, *Standing Rules of Engagement/Standing Rules for the Use of Force for US Forces (U).*

oo. CJCSI 3213.01D, *Joint Operations Security.*

pp. CJCSI 3610.01C, *Aircraft Piracy (Hijacking) and Destruction of Derelict Airborne Objects.*

qq. CJCSI 3710.01B, *DOD Counterdrug Support.*

rr. CJCSI 4120.02C, *Assignment of Movement and Mobility Priority.*

ss. CJCSI 5120.02C, *Joint Doctrine Development System.*

tt. CJCSI 5221.01C, *Delegation of Authority to Commanders of Combatant Commands to Disclose Classified Military Information to Foreign Governments and International Organizations.*

uu. CJCSI 5810.01D, *Implementation of the DOD Law of War Program.*

## 4. Multi-Service Publications

a. FM 3-22.40/NTTP 3-07.3.2/MCWP 3-15.8/AFTTP 3-2.45/USCG Pub 3-07.31, *NLW—Tactical Employment of Non Lethal Weapons.*

b. FM 3-01.1/NTTP 3-26.1.1/AFTTP 3-2.50, *ADUS—Air Defense of the United States (U).*

c. NTTP 3-07.11/CGP 3-07.11, *Maritime Interception Operations.*

d. National Guard Domestic Operations Manual.

**5. Army Publications**

a. Army Doctrine Publication (ADP) 1, *The Army.*

b. ADP 3-0, *Unified Land Operations.*

**6. Navy Publications**

a. Naval Doctrine Publication 1, *Naval Warfare.*

b. NWP 3-10, *Maritime Expeditionary Security Operations.*

c. NWP 3-32, *Maritime Operations at the Operational Level of War.*

d. NTTP 3-32.1, *Maritime Operations Center.*

**7. Marine Corps Publications**

Marine Corps Doctrinal Publication 1, *Warfighting.*

**8. Air Force Publications**

a. Air Force Doctrine Document (AFDD) 1, *Air Force Basic Doctrine, Organization, and Command.*

b. AFDD 3-27, *Homeland Operations.*

c. AFDD 4-02, *Medical Operations.*

d. Air Force Instruction 10-2701, *Organization and Function of the Civil Air Patrol.*

**9. Coast Guard Publications**

a. Coast Guard Publication-1, *US Coast Guard: America's Maritime Guardian.*

b. Coast Guard Publication 3-01, *Maritime Strategy for Homeland Security.*

c. Commandant, United States Coast Guard, Instruction M16247.1, *Maritime Law Enforcement Manual (MLEM).*

# APPENDIX F
## ADMINISTRATIVE INSTRUCTIONS

### 1. User Comments

Users in the field are highly encouraged to submit comments on this publication to: Joint Staff J-7, Deputy Director, Joint Education and Doctrine, ATTN: Joint Doctrine Analysis Division, 116 Lake View Parkway, Suffolk, VA 23435-2697. These comments should address content (accuracy, usefulness, consistency, and organization), writing, and appearance.

### 2. Authorship

The lead agent for this publication is US Northern Command. The Joint Staff doctrine sponsor for this publication is the Director for Operations (J-3).

### 3. Supersession

This publication supersedes JP 3-27, 12 July 2007, *Homeland Defense.*

### 4. Change Recommendations

    a. Recommendations for urgent changes to this publication should be submitted:
       TO:   JOINT STAFF WASHINGTON DC//J7- JE&D//

    b. Routine changes should be submitted electronically to the Deputy Director, Joint Education and Doctrine, ATTN: Joint Doctrine Analysis Division, 116 Lake View Parkway, Suffolk, VA 23435-2697, and info the lead agent and the Director for Joint Force Development, J-7/JE&D.

    c. When a Joint Staff directorate submits a proposal to the CJCS that would change source document information reflected in this publication, that directorate will include a proposed change to this publication as an enclosure to its proposal. The Services and other organizations are requested to notify the Joint Staff J-7 when changes to source documents reflected in this publication are initiated.

### 5. Distribution of Publications

Local reproduction is authorized, and access to unclassified publications is unrestricted. However, access to and reproduction authorization for classified JPs must be IAW DOD Manual 5200.01, Volume 1, *DOD Information Security Program: Overview, Classification, and Declassification,* and DOD Manual 5200.01, Volume 3, *DOD Information Security Program: Protection of Classified Information.*

## 6. Distribution of Electronic Publications

a. Joint Staff J-7 will not print copies of JPs for distribution. Electronic versions are available on JDEIS at https://jdeis.js.mil (NIPRNET) and http://jdeis.js.smil.mil (SIPRNET), and on the JEL at http://www.dtic.mil/doctrine (NIPRNET).

b. Only approved JPs and joint test publications are releasable outside the CCMDs, Services, and Joint Staff. Release of any classified JP to foreign governments or foreign nationals must be requested through the local embassy (Defense Attaché Office) to DIA, Defense Foreign Liaison/IE-3, 200 MacDill Blvd., Joint Base Anacostia-Bolling, Washington, DC 20340-5100.

c. JEL CD-ROM. Upon request of a joint doctrine development community member, the Joint Staff J-7 will produce and deliver one CD-ROM with current JPs. This JEL CD-ROM will be updated not less than semi-annually and when received can be locally reproduced for use within the CCMDs, Services, and combat support agencies.

# GLOSSARY
## PART I—ABBREVIATIONS AND ACRONYMS

| | |
|---|---|
| AC | Active Component |
| ADS | air defense sector |
| AFTTP | Air Force tactics, techniques, and procedures |
| ALCM | air-launched cruise missile |
| ALCOM | United States Alaskan Command |
| AMS | Aerial Measuring System (DOE) |
| ANG | Air National Guard |
| ANR | Alaskan North American Aerospace Defense Command Region |
| AO | area of operations |
| AOR | area of responsibility |
| AOTR | Aviation Operational Threat Response |
| ARG | Accident Response Group (DOE) |
| ARNG | Army National Guard |
| ASD(HD&ASA) | Assistant Secretary of Defense (Homeland Defense and Americas' Security Affairs) |
| ASD(RA) | Assistant Secretary of Defense (Reserve Affairs) |
| AT | antiterrorism |
| ATO | air tasking order |
| | |
| BCC | battle control center |
| BMD | ballistic missile defense |
| BMDS | ballistic missile defense system |
| BSI | base support installation |
| | |
| C2 | command and control |
| CAA | command arrangement agreement |
| CAD | Canadian air division |
| CAISE | civil authority information support element |
| CANR | Canadian North American Aerospace Defense Command Region |
| CANUS | Canada-United States |
| CANUS BDD | Canada-United States Basic Defense Document |
| CANUS CDP | Canada-United States Combined Defense Plan |
| CAP | Civil Air Patrol |
| CBRN | chemical, biological, radiological, and nuclear |
| CBRN CM | chemical, biological, radiological, and nuclear consequence management |
| CCDR | combatant commander |
| CCMD | combatant command |
| CD | counterdrug |
| CDC | Centers for Disease Control and Prevention |
| CDRAFNORTH | Commander, Air Force North |

| | |
|---|---|
| CDRUSAFRICOM | Commander, United States Africa Command |
| CDRNORAD | Commander, North American Aerospace Defense Command |
| CDRUSARNORTH | Commander, United States Army, North |
| CDRUSCENTCOM | Commander, United States Central Command |
| CDRUSELEMNORAD | Commander, United States Element, North American Aerospace Defense Command |
| CDRUSEUCOM | Commander, United States European Command |
| CDRUSNORTHCOM | Commander, United States Northern Command |
| CDRUSPACOM | Commander, United States Pacific Command |
| CDRUSSOCOM | Commander, United States Special Operations Command |
| CDRUSSOUTHCOM | Commander, United States Southern Command |
| CDRUSSTRATCOM | Commander, United States Strategic Command |
| CDRUSTRANSCOM | Commander, United States Transportation Command |
| CDS | Chief of Defence Staff (Canada) |
| CFB | Canadian forces base |
| CG | commanding general |
| CGDEFOR | Coast Guard defense force |
| CGP | Coast Guard publication |
| CI | counterintelligence |
| CI/KR | critical infrastructure and key resources |
| CIO | chief information officer |
| CIP | critical infrastructure protection |
| CJCS | Chairman of the Joint Chiefs of Staff |
| CJCSI | Chairman of the Joint Chiefs of Staff instruction |
| CJOC | Canada Joint Operations Command |
| CJTF | commander, joint task force |
| CM | cruise missile |
| COCOM | combatant command (command authority) |
| COG | continuity of government |
| COIN | counterinsurgency |
| COMPACAF | Commander, Pacific Air Forces |
| COMUSPACFLT | Commander, United States Pacific Fleet |
| CONPLAN | concept plan |
| CONR | continental United States North American Aerospace Defense Command Region |
| CONUS | continental United States |
| COOP | continuity of operations |
| COP | common operational picture |
| CSA | combat support agency |
| CSE | cyberspace support element |
| CSS | combat service support |
| CT | counterterrorism |
| CWMD | countering weapons of mass destruction |

| | |
|---|---|
| DAFL | directive authority for logistics |
| DC3 | Department of Defense Cyber Crime Center |
| DCI | defense critical infrastructure |
| DCIP | Defense Critical Infrastructure Program |
| DCISE | Defense Industrial Base Collaborative Information Sharing Environment |
| DCMA | Defense Contract Management Agency |
| DHS | Department of Homeland Security |
| DIA | Defense Intelligence Agency |
| DIB | defense industrial base |
| DIRLAUTH | direct liaison authorized |
| DISA | Defense Information Systems Agency |
| DLA | Defense Logistics Agency |
| DNDO | Domestic Nuclear Detection Office (DHS) |
| DOD | Department of Defense |
| DODD | Department of Defense directive |
| DODI | Department of Defense instruction |
| DODIN | Department of Defense information networks |
| DOE | Department of Energy |
| DOJ | Department of Justice |
| DOT | Department of Transportation |
| DSCA | defense support of civil authorities |
| DST | Defense Logistics Agency support team |
| DTIP | Disruptive Technology Innovations Partnership (DIA) |
| DTRA | Defense Threat Reduction Agency |
| | |
| EADS | Eastern Air Defense Sector |
| EMIO | expanded maritime interception operations |
| EO | executive order |
| EP | emergency preparedness |
| EXORD | execute order |
| | |
| FAA | Federal Aviation Administration (DOT) |
| FBI | Federal Bureau of Investigation |
| FHP | force health protection |
| FLETC | Federal Law Enforcement Training Center (DHS) |
| FM | field manual (Army) |
| FP | force protection |
| FRMAC | Federal Radiological Monitoring and Assessment Center (DOE) |
| | |
| GCC | geographic combatant commander |
| GEF | Guidance for Employment of the Force |
| GEOINT | geospatial intelligence |
| GMD | ground-based midcourse defense |
| GPS | Global Positioning System |

| | |
|---|---|
| HD | homeland defense |
| HQ | headquarters |
| HS | homeland security |
| HSPD | homeland security Presidential directive |
| | |
| IAMD | integrated air and missile defense |
| IAW | in accordance with |
| IC | intelligence community |
| ICBM | intercontinental ballistic missile |
| IFP | integrated force package |
| IGO | intergovernmental organization |
| IO | information operations |
| IPC | interagency policy committee |
| IRBM | intermediate-range ballistic missile |
| ISR | intelligence, surveillance, and reconnaissance |
| ITW/AA | integrated tactical warning and attack assessment |
| | |
| J-1 | manpower and personnel directorate of a joint staff |
| JADOC | Joint Air Defense Operations Center (NORAD) |
| JCC | joint cyberspace center |
| JCS | Joint Chiefs of Staff |
| JFACC | joint force air component commander |
| JFC | joint force commander |
| JFCC-IMD | Joint Functional Component Command for Integrated Missile Defense |
| JFCC ISR | Joint Functional Component Command for Intelligence, Surveillance, and Reconnaissance (USSTRATCOM) |
| JFCC-Space | Joint Functional Component Command for Space (USSTRATCOM) |
| JFHQ-NCR | Joint Force Headquarters-National Capital Region |
| JFLCC | joint force land component commander |
| JFMCC | joint force maritime component commander |
| JIATF-S | Joint Interagency Task Force-South |
| JOA | joint operations area |
| JP | joint publication |
| JRSOI | joint reception, staging, onward movement, and integration |
| JSR | joint strategy review |
| JTF | joint task force |
| JTF-AK | Joint Task Force-Alaska |
| JTF-CS | Joint Task Force-Civil Support |
| JTF-HD | Joint Task Force-Homeland Defense |
| JTF-N | Joint Task Force-North |
| | |
| LE | law enforcement |
| LEA | law enforcement agency |

| | |
|---|---|
| LFA | lead federal agency |
| LNO | liaison officer |
| | |
| MA | mortuary affairs |
| MASINT | measurement and signature intelligence |
| MCM | mine countermeasures |
| MCWP | Marine Corps warfighting publication |
| MDA | Missile Defense Agency |
| MHD | maritime homeland defense |
| MHS | maritime homeland security |
| MIO | maritime interception operations |
| MISO | military information support operations |
| MOA | memorandum of agreement |
| MOTR | maritime operational threat response |
| MOU | memorandum of understanding |
| MRBM | medium-range ballistic missile |
| | |
| NARAC | National Atmospheric Release Advisory Center (DOE) |
| NCIJTF-AG | National Cyber Investigative Joint Task Force-Analytical Group (DOD) |
| NCR | National Capital Region (US) |
| NCRCC | National Capital Region Coordination Center |
| NCR-IADS | National Capital Region–Integrated Air Defense System |
| NCSD | National Cybe Security Division (DHS) |
| NCTC | National Counterterrorism Center |
| NDHQ | National Defence Headquarters, Canada |
| NDDOC | North American Aerospace Defense Command and United States Northern Command Deployment and Distribution Operations Cell |
| NEST | nuclear emergency support team (DOE) |
| NG | National Guard |
| NGA | National Geospatial-Intelligence Agency |
| NGB | National Guard Bureau |
| NG JFHQ-State | National Guard joint force headquarters-state |
| NGO | nongovernmental organization |
| NMS | national military strategy |
| NNSA | National Nuclear Security Administration (DOE) |
| NORAD | North American Aerospace Defense Command |
| NPPD | National Protection and Programs Directorate (DHS) |
| NRF | National Response Framework |
| NSA | National Security Agency |
| NSC | National Security Council |
| NSC/DC | National Security Council/Deputies Committee |
| NSC/PC | National Security Council/Principals Committee |
| NSMS | National Strategy for Maritime Security |
| NSPD | national security Presidential directive |

| | |
|---|---|
| NSS | national security strategy |
| NST | National Geospatial-Intelligence Agency support team |
| NTTP | Navy tactics, techniques, and procedures |
| NVDT | National Geospatial-Intelligence Agency voluntary deployment team |
| NWP | Navy warfare publication |
| | |
| OA | operational area |
| ONE | Operation NOBLE EAGLE |
| OPCON | operational control |
| OPLAN | operation plan |
| OPSEC | operations security |
| | |
| PA | public affairs |
| PCA | Posse Comitatus Act |
| PDD | Presidential decision directive |
| PI | pandemic influenza |
| PN | partner nation |
| PPD | Presidential policy directive |
| | |
| QRF | quick response force |
| | |
| RAP | Radiological Assistance Program (DOE) |
| RC | Reserve Component |
| REAC/TS | radiation emergency assistance center/training site (DOE) |
| RFF | request for forces |
| ROE | rules of engagement |
| RRF | rapid response force |
| RS | religious support |
| RST | religious support team |
| RUF | rules for the use of force |
| | |
| SATCOM | satellite communications |
| SCA | space coordinating authority |
| SCC-WMD | United States Strategic Command Center for Combating Weapons of Mass Destruction |
| SecDef | Secretary of Defense |
| SIGINT | signals intelligence |
| SIOC | Strategic Information and Operations Center (FBI) |
| SIR | Strategic Military Intelligence Review |
| SLCM | sea-launched cruise missile |
| SO | special operations |
| SOCPAC | Special Operations Command, Pacific |
| SOF | special operations forces |
| SPP | State Partnership Program (NG) |
| SRBM | short-range ballistic missile |

| | |
|---|---|
| SROE | standing rules of engagement |
| SRUF | standing rules for the use of force |
| | |
| TAA | tactical assembly area |
| TACON | tactical control |
| TAG | the adjutant general |
| TCO | transnational criminal organization |
| TSA | Transportation Security Administration (DHS) |
| TSC | theater security cooperation |
| TSOC | theater special operations command |
| | |
| UCP | Unified Command Plan |
| USAF | United States Air Force |
| USARNORTH | United States Army, North |
| USARPAC | United States Army, Pacific Command |
| USC | United States Code |
| USCG | United States Coast Guard |
| USCYBERCOM | United States Cyber Command |
| USD(P) | Under Secretary of Defense for Policy |
| USELEMNORAD | United States Element, North American Aerospace Defense Command |
| USEUCOM | United States European Command |
| USG | United States Government |
| USMARFORNORTH | United States Marine Corps Forces North |
| USN | United States Navy |
| USNORTHCOM | United States Northern Command |
| USPACOM | United States Pacific Command |
| USSOUTHCOM | United States Southern Command |
| USSTRATCOM | United States Strategic Command |
| USTRANSCOM | United States Transportation Command |
| | |
| WADS | Western Air Defense Sector |
| WMD | weapons of mass destruction |
| WRA | weapons release authority |

## PART II—TERMS AND DEFINITIONS

**aerospace defense.** 1. All defensive measures designed to destroy or nullify attacking enemy aircraft and missiles and also negate hostile space systems. 2. An inclusive term encompassing air defense, ballistic missile defense, and space defense. (JP 1-02. SOURCE: JP 3-27)

**air sovereignty.** A nation's inherent right to exercise absolute control and authority over the airspace above its territory. (Approved for incorporation into JP 1-02 with JP 3-27 as the source JP.)

**air sovereignty mission.** None. (Approved for removal from JP 1-02.)

**civil defense.** None. (Approved for removal from JP 1-02.)

**civil defense emergency.** None. (Approved for removal from JP 1-02.)

**civil requirements.** None. (Approved for removal from JP 1-02.)

**civil transportation.** None. (Approved for removal from JP 1-02.)

**critical infrastructure and key resources.** The infrastructure and assets vital to a nation's security, governance, public health and safety, economy, and public confidence. Also called **CI/KR.** (Approved for inclusion in JP 1-02.)

**defense critical infrastructure.** Department of Defense and non-Department of Defense networked assets and facilities essential to project, support, and sustain military forces and operations worldwide. Also called **DCI.** (Approved for incorporation into JP 1-02.)

**defense emergency.** None. (Approved for removal from JP 1-02.)

**defense industrial base.** The Department of Defense, government, and private sector worldwide industrial complex with capabilities to perform research and development, design, produce, and maintain military weapon systems, subsystems, components, or parts to meet military requirements. Also called **DIB.** (Approved for incorporation into JP 1-02.)

**domestic emergencies.** Civil defense emergencies, civil disturbances, major disasters, or natural disasters affecting the public welfare and occurring within the United States and its territories. (Approved for incorporation into JP 1-02.)

**global strike.** None. (Upon approval of this revised publication, this term and its definition will be removed from JP 1-02.)

**homeland defense.** The protection of United States sovereignty, territory, domestic population, and critical infrastructure against external threats and aggression or other threats as directed by the President. Also called **HD.** (Approved for incorporation into JP 1-02.)

**homeland security.** A concerted national effort to prevent terrorist attacks within the United States; reduce America's vulnerability to terrorism, major disasters, and other emergencies; and minimize the damage and recover from attacks, major disasters, and other emergencies that occur. Also called **HS.** (Approved for incorporation into JP 1-02 with JP 3-27 as the source JP.)

**major disaster.** None. (Approved for removal from JP 1-02.)

**quick response force.** None. (Approved for removal from JP 1-02.)

**rapid response force.** None. (Approved for removal from JP 1-02.)

Intentionally Blank

# JOINT DOCTRINE PUBLICATIONS HIERARCHY

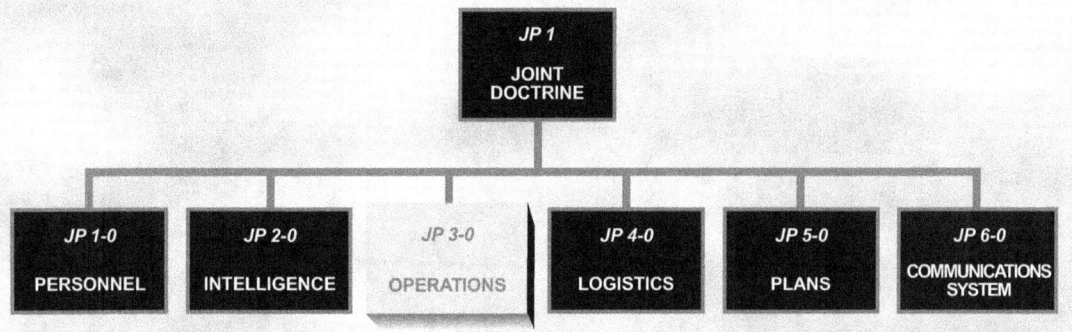

| JP 1 — JOINT DOCTRINE | | | | | |
|---|---|---|---|---|---|
| **JP 1-0**<br>PERSONNEL | **JP 2-0**<br>INTELLIGENCE | **JP 3-0**<br>OPERATIONS | **JP 4-0**<br>LOGISTICS | **JP 5-0**<br>PLANS | **JP 6-0**<br>COMMUNICATIONS SYSTEM |

All joint publications are organized into a comprehensive hierarchy as shown in the chart above. **Joint Publication (JP) 3-27** is in the **Operations** series of joint doctrine publications. The diagram below illustrates an overview of the development process:

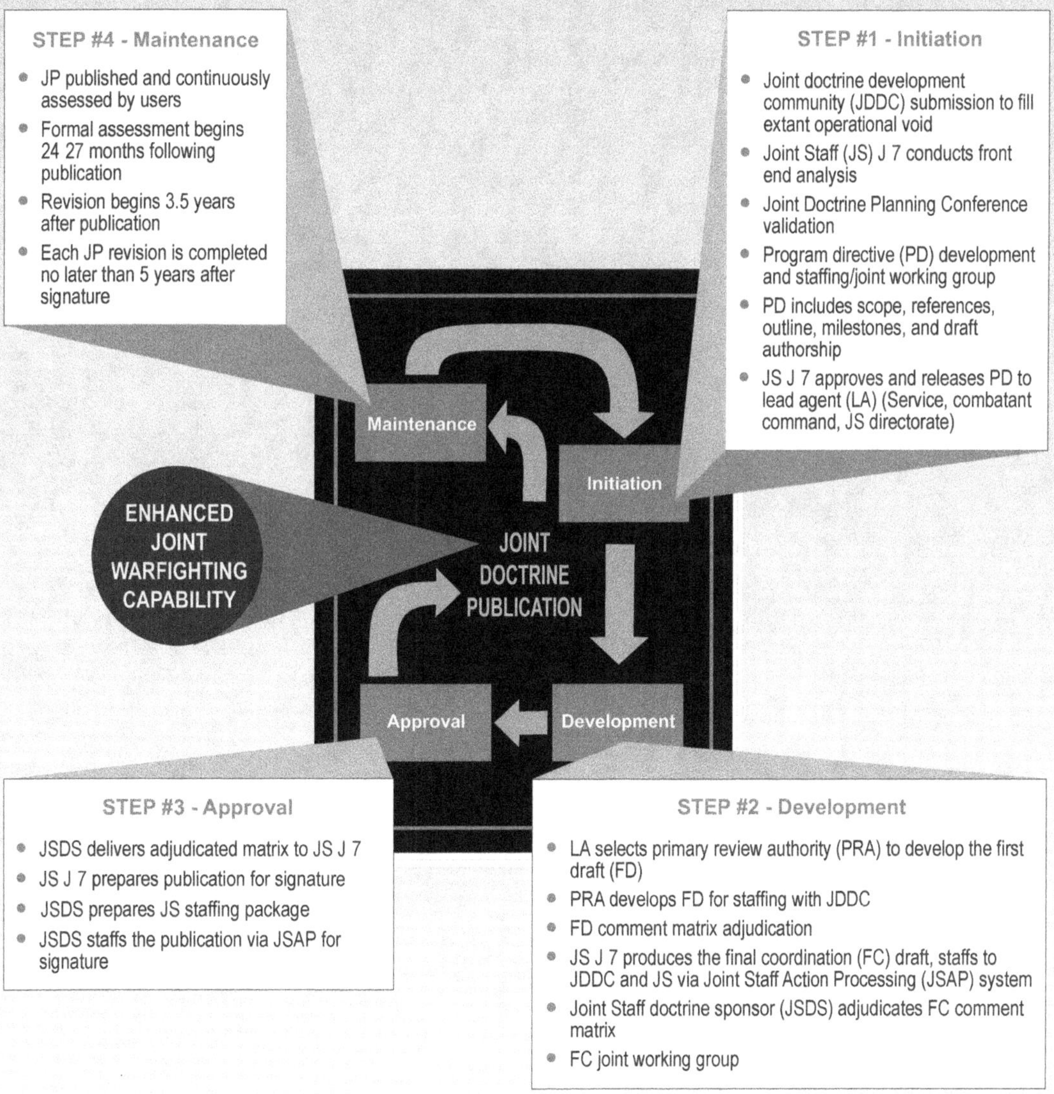

## STEP #4 - Maintenance

- JP published and continuously assessed by users
- Formal assessment begins 24 27 months following publication
- Revision begins 3.5 years after publication
- Each JP revision is completed no later than 5 years after signature

## STEP #1 - Initiation

- Joint doctrine development community (JDDC) submission to fill extant operational void
- Joint Staff (JS) J 7 conducts front end analysis
- Joint Doctrine Planning Conference validation
- Program directive (PD) development and staffing/joint working group
- PD includes scope, references, outline, milestones, and draft authorship
- JS J 7 approves and releases PD to lead agent (LA) (Service, combatant command, JS directorate)

**ENHANCED JOINT WARFIGHTING CAPABILITY**

**JOINT DOCTRINE PUBLICATION**

Maintenance · Initiation · Development · Approval

## STEP #3 - Approval

- JSDS delivers adjudicated matrix to JS J 7
- JS J 7 prepares publication for signature
- JSDS prepares JS staffing package
- JSDS staffs the publication via JSAP for signature

## STEP #2 - Development

- LA selects primary review authority (PRA) to develop the first draft (FD)
- PRA develops FD for staffing with JDDC
- FD comment matrix adjudication
- JS J 7 produces the final coordination (FC) draft, staffs to JDDC and JS via Joint Staff Action Processing (JSAP) system
- Joint Staff doctrine sponsor (JSDS) adjudicates FC comment matrix
- FC joint working group

www.ingramcontent.com/pod-product-compliance
Lightning Source LLC
Chambersburg PA
CBHW081829280526
45789CB00007B/2392